Truth for the Good Life

Robert P. Lightner

AF864803

MEMBER OF
EVANGELICAL CHRISTIAN
PUBLISHERS ASSOCIATION

ACCENT BOOKS
A division of Accent-B/P Publications
12100 W. Sixth Avenue
P.O. Box 15337
Denver, Colorado 80215

Copyright © 1978 Accent-B/P Publications, Inc.
Printed in U.S.A.

All rights reserved. No portion of this book may be reproduced in any form without the written permission of the publishers, with the exception of brief excerpts in magazine reviews.

Library of Congress Number: 77-81776

ISBN 0-916406-71-7

Dedicated to

**my wife Pearl and
our daughters Nancy Kay,
Nadine Pearl and
Natalie Sue who share
with me in the good life.**

FOREWORD

Life in Christ is the good life. "It's a wonderful, wonderful life," not because it is free of problems, but because we enjoy His love and care as we pilgrim on toward the Promised Land.

Also, as Robert Lightner points out, the good life is good because it comes from God and He is good. It is life based upon truth and lived according to truth, God's truth. Apart from God life is so impoverished!

I feel this book will help those who have the good life to better understand the truth upon which it is based. It is my sincere desire that as you read you will see more clearly how God's truth relates to life at its best. And, if you have not yet come to experience this, I would strongly encourage you to pray, "Lord, *give me the good life.*"

John W Peterson

CONTENTS

Chapter One
It's Still the Truth

Up until rather recent years, most of those who did not believe the Bible to be God's Word were outside the church. It's different today, however. Some of the Bible's fiercest critics are in positions of religious leadership. True, many people outside organized religion still reject the inspiration and authority of the Bible, but added to their number are many others who present themselves as servants of Christ. Foes of the Bible, in other words, are turning up in strange places these days.

We are told again and again by many that it is time for a new view of the Bible. The position held by the church from its beginning is no longer relevant in our highly scientific and sophisticated age, these people insist. But just what has been the prevailing view of the church toward the Bible? Since we are urged to set this view aside, we first need to know what it is. Then we can decide whether or not to do as we are told.

A brief sampling of views from the early church fathers will illustrate the historic view of the church with regard to the Bible. Clement of Alexandria was emphatic in saying that not even a jot or tittle of Scripture could disappear, because all had indeed been spoken by the mouth of the Lord. Gregory of Nazianzus insisted that "even the smallest lines in Scripture are due to the minute care of the Holy Spirit." St. Augustine wrote, "Let us give in and yield our assent to the authority of Holy Scripture, which knows not how either to be deceived or to deceive." Origen put it this way: "The sacred Scriptures come from the fulness of the Spirit, so that there is nothing in the prophets, or the law, or the gospel, or the apostles which descends not from the fulness of the Divine Majesty."

Benjamin Breckinridge Warfield, an astute student of history and of the Bible, made this summary observation of the historic Christian view of Scripture in *The Inspiration and Authority of the Bible*: "What this church doctrine is, it is scarcely necessary minutely to describe. It will suffice to remind ourselves that it looks upon the Bible as an oracular book—as the Word of God in such a sense that whatever it says God says—not a book, then, in which one may, by searching, find some word of God, but a book which may be frankly appealed to at any point with the assurance that whatever it may be found to say, that is the Word of God."

One of the great emphases of the sixteenth-century Protestant Reformation was the insistence of the Reformers upon *sola Scriptura* ("the Scripture alone") as the only infallible authority. An exalted view of the Bible was held by all the Reformers. Who would question that out of the Reformation came an attitude that the Bible is open for all and authoritative in all?

What, then, was the historic Christian position about the Bible? It was simply this: the Bible is God's inspired Word. It was breathed out by Him. He protected and controlled the human writers so that they were kept from all error and from all omission and addition as they recorded God's Word. Is this view of the traditional church position concerning the Bible merely the biased testimony of those who want to find support for their own view? No. Even those who reject the historic Christian position agree on what that position was. "Scripture . . . was accepted by Christendom with practical unanimity from the second century to the nineteenth," according to Cecil Cadoux, in *The Case for Evangelical Modernism*.

In the mid-nineteenth century, concurrent with the development of what has come to be called the "higher critical view of the Bible," the historic Christian view was abandoned by many.

The higher critical view was really the result of applying the Darwinian theory of evolution to the Bible. Higher critics attempted to discern the origin of the ideas set forth in the Bible. Soon they began to "determine" at what points and to what extent the Bible was true.

The view of the Bible set forth by these higher critics was diametrically opposed to the historic Christian view. The prevailing view of the higher critics was that the Bible was composed of nothing more than myths and legends. Those who held this view rearranged and redated many books of the Bible in order to make Scripture conform to their claim that it is not the Word of God. They insisted that the books and passages which claim to tell the future had been written after the events they "predicted" occurred.

Today there are still some who hold to the view described above, which we might call the "old classic liberal" view. But far more popular in liberal circles today is a view which, though it is very similar to the old view, does speak of the Bible with more reverence and seriousness. This view is the result of the attempt to "rediscover" the Bible, to have a "Biblical theology." On quick impulse you might ask, "But what is wrong with rediscovering the Bible and having a Biblical theology?"

Well, in the first place, the Bible has not been lost. And then we might ask, Is the Bible really being rediscovered even by those who consider it to be lost? And, is there really a return to "Biblical theology"? After a careful survey, it is easy to see that the Bible being rediscovered is not the Bible of historic Christianity; and the result of this "rediscovery" is not a Biblical theology.

The fact is, the view of the Bible held by those "rediscovering" it is not as open and honest as the old liberal view it is seeking to replace. In other words, the same higher critical view is embraced, but it is presented in words and ways which deceptively make it look like the historic Christian view. Today's higher critics do not deny the Bible's inspiration and authority as openly and as obviously as higher critics once did. According to *"Fundamentalism" and the Word of God,* by J. I. Packer, "The new Liberals are anxious to be biblical in their beliefs, and condemn old Liberalism as heretical; but they are held back from a consistently biblical outlook by the legacy of rationalistic criticism which they have inherited . . . The self-contradictory character of liberal Christianity has never become more evident than here. . . . The truth is that 'Biblical Theology' wants to have it both ways. . . . It wants to be able to commend itself to the world as scientific, because it holds to the unorthodox views of nineteenth century critics, and to the Church as Christian, because it deals with 'the biblical point of view.'"

The comments of G. Bromley Oxnam, one from the "rediscover the Bible," "Biblical Theology" school of thought, will reveal how far removed these views are from the historic Christian position. In *A Testament of Faith* Oxnam claims, "The revelation was conditioned by their ability to understand, and their reports bear evidence of the limitations that current events, and current practice evoke. Take the cosmology accepted by the Old Testament writers, for instance; or the belief in demons; or Paul's attitude toward women. To hold that Paul's advice on women is truth revealed by God and binding upon all is as sorry as to hold that God commanded the Jews to commit atrocities on their enemies in war. Nonetheless truth is revealed."

This view is not Oxnam's alone. Speaking of the Bible in *The Case for Theology in Liberal Perspective,* L. Harold DeWolf comments, "In it are to be found the erring words of men as well as the authoritative word of God."

A third modern view of the Bible, also at variance with the historic Christian view, is really hardly distinguishable from the views described above. "The Bible is not the Word of God, but it may become the Word of God to and for an individual" is the basic idea of this view.

God's Word is thought of as a record of revelation or a witness to it, but is not considered to be revelation itself. In *Thy Word Is Truth,* Edward J. Young states, "According to this modern view the authority of the Bible does not at all reside in itself; it resides rather in the fact that when the truth of the Bible meets me in a Divine human encounter, then, in that particular case, the Bible becomes the Word of God for me."

In the last few years another view has developed, this time among those who say they believe the Bible is inspired. These people say that when the Bible speaks about its major theme, salvation and the Christian life, it is without error. But, they claim, when the Bible touches upon matters which are not directly related to its central theme but are peripheral matters, it must not be expected to be without error. The attempt of those who hold this view is to distinguish between inspiration and inerrancy.

By now it should be obvious to us that the modern views of the Bible are in sharp disagreement with the historic Christian view. We will further see that these views are also out of harmony with the Bible's own witness and the claims of Christ as well.

How we wish to respond to the evidence is,of course,a personal matter. But there is no way to escape the fact that literally hundreds of times the Bible claims to be the Word of God. Whatever view of the Bible we may hold to, we must take these claims into account. Either we will receive and believe them as valid, or we must ignore or flatly deny them as being lies. Of course if the Bible can't be believed when it speaks about itself, then there is no reason to believe it when it speaks about anything else. But let's first examine the evidence before passing judgment.

"All scripture is given by inspiration of God," Paul told young Timothy (II Timothy 3:16). The apostle was referring primarily to the Old Testament, for at this time the New Testament was not yet completed. But as it was completed it, too, could be, and was, classified as "inspired." The entire Bible is God's recorded revelation. He is its source. All Scripture originated with Him. He literally breathed it out. In some instances the human writers were dictated to—told precisely what words to write; other times they were not. Each writer used his own style to record God's Word; yet what he wrote was exactly what God wanted written. The Bible was, and is, God's Word, given by "inspiration."

God did not prompt those who wrote the Bible by simply giving them noble ideas to write about, and then place His stamp of approval upon the product. No, the Greek word translated "inspiration" does not mean that. In fact, "inspiration" is really not the best rendering of the original language. "Inspiration of God" comes from one word which literally means "the breath of God." So that is what Paul is calling all Scripture: the breath of God. And unless we believe God is capable of lying or making mistakes, we must take this to mean that the Bible is without error.

Nowhere does the Bible make any effort to deny or even ignore the fact that men with all the frailities common to humanity wrote Scripture. But Scripture does tell us that the human penmen were supernaturally protected as they wrote God's Word. According to the Apostle Peter, "The prophecy came not in old time by the will of man: but holy men of God spake as they were moved by the Holy Ghost" (II Peter 1:21).

Peter further declares that "no prophecy of the scripture is of any private interpretation" (II Peter 1:20). By this he means no Scripture came into being as a result of the investigation or reason of man. It didn't come "by the will of man." It didn't have its origin with man.

Peter points out that the men who wrote Scripture were "moved" or "borne along" by the Holy Spirit. In *Thy Word Is Truth,* Edward J. Young explains it this way: "The men who spake from God are said to have been borne by the Holy Spirit. That is, the Spirit actually lifted them up and carried them along, and thus they spake. They were borne or carried along under the power of the Spirit and not by their own power. That which is picked up and borne, however, is absolutely passive. So the writers of Scripture who spake from God were passive. It was the Spirit of God who bore them. It was He who was active, and they who were passive. Thus He bore them to the goal of His own desiring."

In studying the Bible's view of itself, it also becomes clear that both Old and New Testaments are equally inspired of God. We see this in Paul's exhortation to Timothy concerning elders and church leaders. To defend his point that these men were to be treated kindly and paid fairly, Paul quoted two passages, referring to both as Scripture (I Timothy 5:18). From the Old Testament he quoted, "Thou shalt not muzzle the ox that treadeth out the corn" (cf. Deuteronomy 25:4). And from the New Testament he quoted, "The labourer is worthy of his hire" (cf. Luke 10:7).

The important thing to notice here is that Paul called both of these passages Scripture. There was no doubt in his mind that both Old and New Testaments were inspired of God, the very "breath of God."

In addition to the major passages discussed above there are literally hundreds of other passages which reveal the Bible's view of itself. Phrases like "the word of the Lord came unto me saying," "Jehovah spoke by me saying," "thus saith the Lord," and "the Spirit of the Lord spoke by me" abound in Scripture. "The law of the Lord is perfect," wrote the psalmist (Psalm 19:7) And again he wrote, "the words of the Lord are pure words" (Psalm 12:6). The Word of God claims to be forever settled in Heaven (Psalm 119:89). It also claims to be true from the beginning (Psalm 119:160).

Not only does Scripture itself claim to be perfect, but throughout His public ministry Christ also mentioned Scripture constantly and continually, saying that the Scriptures were the very "commandment of God" (Mark 7:8,9). He further claimed that Scripture was the product of the Holy Spirit (Mark 12:36). For Christ, Scripture possessed a durable, eternal quality (Matthew 5:17,18; 24:35). It was inviolable and divinely authoritative (John 10:35). With broad, sweeping statements the Saviour embraced and taught the inspiration and authority of the entire Old Testament (Luke 24:44).

As far as Christ was concerned, the entire Old Testament was inspired of God. He frequently referred to the threefold Jewish division—law, prophets, and Psalms—as being from God (cf. Luke 24:44). This threefold division embraced all the same books that are now in our Old Testament. Therefore, since what Christ saw as God-breathed and unerring is the same Scripture we have today, the

Old Testament is still God-breathed, still unerring.

The Saviour also appealed to individual parts of Scripture, giving them the same high regard He gave the whole. But even specifically, He accepted the very words of Scripture as being divinely binding. Christ's view of Scripture was that of verbal inspiration, not just thought or concept inspiration. In fact, in some instances the validity of His entire argument depended upon the authority of one word (Matthew 22:23-33; 22:43,44). Jesus taught that even the letters and smallest markings which make up words were inspired of God. Not even a "jot" or a "tittle," tiny elements of the Hebrew language, would pass away without being fulfilled (Matthew 5:17,18). In fact, even the tense and number of the grammatical construction used to express God's truth were inspired (Matthew 22:32; John 10:34).

"But," someone will say, "what Christ said about the Scripture applied only to the Old Testament." It is true that the New Testament was not yet written when our Saviour ministered on earth. And what He said did relate specifically to the Old Testament. However, His teaching of the inspiration of the Old Testament may be applied to the New Testament as well.

The Saviour stood between the Old and New Testaments. In anticipation He guaranteed the full inspiration of the New

Testament, prophesying what the New Testament later reported to have happened. For instance, in His parting words to His disciples, Christ promised to send the Holy Spirit to continue the work He had begun. "But the Comforter, which is the Holy Ghost, whom the Father will send in my name, he shall teach you all things, and bring all things to your remembrance, whatsoever I have said unto you" (John 14:26). It is clear from the New Testament that the Holy Spirit did come and do what Christ said He would do (I Corinthians 2:9-12; II Peter 3:1,2; Revelation 1:1,2). Therefore, in prophesying what the New Testament would later claim to be true, Christ was teaching the inspiration of the New Testament.

There you have it: the historic Christian view of the Bible, modern views at variance with it, the Bible's view of itself, and Christ's view.

Does it really matter all that much how the Bible is approached? How does my view of the Bible relate to my everyday life, anyway? Is there any relation between how I view the Bible and how I wage the battle of life?

Of course it matters how I view the Bible. Indeed there is a relation between what I believe about the Bible and how I live. I must live either under the authority of God or under the authority of man. There simply can be no other source of authority for me to follow. And if the

Bible is not God's Word, it is not authoritative. Therefore I must follow the authority of man.

In addition to affecting my lifestyle, my view of the Bible will reflect my view of God, whether I want it to or not. After all, in the Bible God does claim that Scripture is indeed His Word. If it isn't, even in the smallest portion, then God has not told us the truth, and consequently He can't be trusted. And if I can't trust what God said about the Bible, how can I trust anything He has said? I can't! But since the Bible is God's Word, I can trust it and I can trust its Author.

Embracing the Bible's view of itself ought to make a profound difference in my life. I need to do more than just give an academic nod to its teaching. I need to live according to Scripture—submitting to its authority, subjecting myself to it, and obeying it. Since my Saviour accepted, believed, and obeyed Scripture, it seems only right that I, too, respond to the Bible as the God-breathed, inerrant Book it claims to be.

Chapter Two
The God of the Bible

What could possibly be more central to the Christian faith than belief in the God of the Bible? Nothing! Those who profess to be Christians, and even those who do not—all give evidence of interest in God and have questions about Him. But there must be no mistaking it—Christians and non-Christians have entirely different concepts of God.

There is a good deal of "God-talk" going on in our highly secularized and materialistic age. But the question is, How much of the talk about God is really related to the God and Father of our Lord Jesus Christ, the God of holy Scripture? When the Biblical portraits of God and the popular talk about God are compared, we get the impression that there is little relationship between the two.

What, then, is the Bible's teaching about God? Does He really exist? If He does, How does He exist? How may we describe Him? What is He doing? What difference should accepting the God of Scripture make in my life? These are the questions we need to have answered from God's Word.

The Bible begins with the grand assumption that God is. "In the beginning God"—these opening words of Scripture are without doubt the most basic, yet the most important, words ever uttered. Here we have not an argument or defense for God's existence, but a sublime declaration assuming and affirming the reality of His existence. And the same is true all through the Bible.

Neither does the Bible give us a definition of God. Perhaps the closest thing to definitions would be the expressions penned by John: "God is light" (I John 1:5); "God is love" (I John 4:8); God is "eternal life" (I John 5:20). God is all these and more. But is it really possible to *define* God? No; not if by "define" you mean "describe fully." God will not, and cannot, be boxed in like that. But, yes, He can be defined if by "define" you mean describe so as to distinguish from all else and all others. God is indeed unique, comparable to no one else.

Before we look at the Biblical evidence for the existence of God, let's think about what might be called *reasonable evidence* that God exists. In the final analysis these arguments do not really "prove" the existence of God, but they do supply reasonable evidence for His existence. There are basically four of these arguments.

The first one goes something like this: The world we live in must be explained by a cause adequate to have produced it. After all, the argument goes, every effect must have an adequate cause. Where did the world come from? The cause of all things must be greater than the effect. There must have been a first cause, a first mover capable of bringing the world into existence.

And then when we look a bit more closely at our world, we see precise order and intricate design. This is the basis for the second rational argument. The existence of the world argues for a powerful first cause; the intricate complexity and design in that world argues for an intelligent, rational and purposeful first cause. Only a fool would look at an intricate mechanism of any kind, let alone the world, and say it came into existence by chance.

Another step in the path of reasonable evidence for God's existence relates to man himself. In our world of intricate design and complexity is man, who is himself a specific example of that intricacy and complexity. Man possesses personality and intelligence; so surely an impersonal and unintelligent power did not bring such a being into existence.

Finally, we need to realize that all men

everywhere possess in their minds an idea of God. That is, all have, from birth, a concept of right and wrong and, consequently, of a perfect Being. Where did man get such a notion? As the argument goes—all men have the idea of a perfect Being because there is, in fact, such a Being.

What of the Biblical evidence for God's existence? You will recall that at the beginning of this discussion we noted that the Bible opens with the assumption of God's existence. It does not debate or try to argue that He is. And yet holy Scripture does present irrefutable evidence that God is, that He has worked, and that He is working in His world. This is extremely important to understand, for he who would come to God must believe that He is. He must be our starting point. This is precisely what Hebrews 11:6 conveys: "Without faith it is impossible to please him; for he that cometh to God must believe that he is."

Without doubt the strongest evidence in the Bible for God's existence comes from its testimony about the Lord Jesus Christ. He came to the earth to reveal God. "No man hath seen God at any time; the only begotten Son, which is in the bosom of the Father, he hath declared him" (John 1:18). The Saviour exposed God to the world, for He is the mirror Image of the Father. In Him, Paul declares, "dwelleth all the fulness of the Godhead bodily"

(Colossians 2:9). Therefore, Christ could rightly say to Philip, "He that hath seen me hath seen the Father" (John 14:9).

We Christians worship one God. We believe firmly the message God gave to Israel of old, "Hear, O Israel: the Lord our God is one Lord" (Deuteronomy 6:4).

Christians believe also in a personal God. The God of the Bible is not a mere power, force or influence. He possesses intellect, emotion and will. There are great depths to the "wisdom and knowledge of God! How unsearchable are his judgments, and his ways past finding out!" (Romans 11:33). The same God has the ability of self-determination or will, too. He is "not willing that any should perish, but that all should come to repentance" (II Peter 3:9).

God's great attributes or characteristics also indicate the existence of His personality. Only a person can exercise love, grace, mercy, all knowledge, and all power. Further indication that God is a Person is that personal pronouns are used with reference to God throughout the Bible. Our God is not merely an abstract, elusive "power," but a personal, loving God. He possesses all the elements of personality in perfection. It is a great comfort to know God is a person, for He is the One with whom every child of God can have fellowship. In fact, He longs to have fellowship with each of His children.

The Bible presents the one God as existing in holy Trinity. What does this mean? It means that the one true God manifests Himself in three persons—God the Father, God the Son, and God the Holy Spirit. The Bible clearly teaches this concept of the Trinity without even using the word "Trinity."

In the Old Testament there are implications of more than one person in the Godhead. One of the names used of God, *Elohim,* is a plural form in the Hebrew. Interestingly, it is used and translated "God" in the very passage which stresses the oneness of God (Deuteronomy 6:4). Plural pronouns are also used of God (Genesis 1:26; 3:22).

In the Bible there is a distinction between the "Lord" or Jehovah-God and His "anointed" or Christ (Psalm 2). And in Psalm 139:7 David clearly refers to the Holy Spirit. So, you can see that there is the repeated emphasis upon a plurality in the Godhead. But the Old Testament goes even further than that. There are implications of not just a plurality but of a specific number of three persons making up the Godhead (see Numbers 6:24-27; Isaiah 48:16; 63:7-10).

And what of the New Testament? It is even more specific in its teaching. Three persons are called God (John 1:1,14; 6:27; Acts 5:3-9), although each is seen as a distinct person. And although they are distinct, the members of the Godhead are equal in deity, being associated with each other (Matthew 28:19,20).

In the account of our Lord's baptism at the hands of John, we see evidence of the Trinity. The Son was baptized, the Spirit descended in the form of a dove, and the Father spoke from Heaven (Matthew 3:13-17).

In His upper room discourse on the eve of His death, Jesus told His disciples of the coming Holy Spirit. This Holy Spirit, He said, would come from the Father in the Son's name (John 14:16, 26).

In his closing benediction to the Christians in Corinth, Paul refers to "the grace of the Lord Jesus Christ, and the love of God, and the communion of the Holy Ghost" (II Corinthians 13:14).

Supernatural? Yes. A Mystery? Yes. But nevertheless, we believe the central doctrine of the Trinity because it finds its basis in Scripture. And we agree with Augustine, the fifth-century church father, who said of the Trinity: "In no other subject is error more dangerous or inquiry more laborious, or discovery of the truth more profitable."

Does any believer need to be convinced that God is sovereign? I really doubt it. After all, when true believers pray they acknowledge that God is in control and able to help them and others. Those who know and love the Lord often thank Him for their salvation. And every time they do, they give consent to God's sovereign work of grace in their hearts and lives. If we have any burden at all for our unregenerate relatives, our friends, and the masses of the world, we pray for their salvation. When we do, we are, in effect, saying, "God, I know you are sovereign so I trust you to break men's stubborn will and save them."

Hannah, Samuel's mother, readily acknowledged God as the absolute and sole ruler when she proclaimed that He raises up and takes down as He pleases (I Samuel 2:2-8). David, the king, also acknowledged God's sovereignty as he defended the total lordship of Jehovah-God (I Chronicles 29:11,12). The Lord Jesus said of His Father, He is "greater than all" (John 10:29). The Apostle Paul penned the greatest treatise ever written on the sovereignty of God (Romans 9—11). To the Ephesians he said God works "all things after the counsel of his own will" (Ephesians 1:11).

Paul sensed the marvel and mystery of God's sovereignty. And his words of praise should be ours. "O the depth of the riches both of the wisdom and knowledge of God! how unsearchable are his judgments, and his ways past finding out! For who hath known the mind of the Lord? or who hath been his counsellor? Or who hath first given to him, and it shall be recompensed unto him again? For of him, and through him, and to him are all things: to whom be glory for ever. Amen" (Romans 11:33-36).

Is there not some way for us to describe God? Yes, a description of Him is realized when we observe His characteristics as they are set forth in the Bible. These reveal God's nature. And an understanding of them will keep us from viewing Him as a bearded, benevolent old grandfather, or as a sort of super power or influence in the world.

These characteristics or qualities of God are often called His attributes. They might also be viewed as perfections in God. Whatever one wishes to call them, they describe the nature of God and His activity. It is impossible to think of God apart from His perfections, for He never existed apart from them. They always belonged to Him. And yet He is more than them all. In his *Systematic Theology,* Lewis Sperry Chafer described their relation to God and His to them this way: "The whole of the divine essence is in each attribute, and the attribute belongs to the whole essence. The attributes belong eternally to the essence."

Every effort must have an adequate cause to account for it, *except* with God. He possesses in Himself the ground of His own existence. In the absolute sense, He possesses life; He does not depend on anyone or anything outside of Himself for life. "The Father hath life in himself" (John 5:26). God's independence is really the basis for man's dependence upon Him for everything.

Man is, of course, very finite. But God is infinite. He is not bound by the limitations so common to man. Since He is not limited by time, God is eternal. He is "the everlasting God" (Genesis 21:33). Neither is our God restricted by space. He is beyond all spatial limitations.

Since God does not possess a physical body, He is Spirit (John 4:24). The only physical body God has is the believer's. By His Spirit He dwells in each believer (I Corinthians 6:19). How terribly important it is, then, for each child of God to present his body as a living sacrifice to God (Romans 12:1).

Our God is changeless, too. That is, He never changes in His essence, His character or His nature (Malachi 3:6; James 1:17). Bound only by Himself, God is now and always will be all He has been from all eternity.

"The Lord our God is holy" (Psalm 99:9). This does not mean He has arrived at a state of perfection. Neither does it mean He struggles to maintain it. He has always been, and always will be, holy, and His dealings with Satan and sin do not in any way affect His holiness.

Love is not God, contrary to the impression many people give today. But God is love (I John 4:8). This means more than just that He loves. He does love, to be sure. But God's love is not merely something He possesses. It is what He is!

Closely associated with God's love is the

fact that "the Lord is merciful and gracious" (Psalm 103:8). Because He is merciful, God withholds deserved punishment. Because He is gracious He bestows undeserved favor.

God knows, He comprehends all things. Without having to discover facts, God possesses perfect knowledge (Isaiah 40:13,14; Romans 11:34-36). The future and the past are all known by God just as fully as the present is known.

God is present everywhere at the same time. No one can hide from Him. Before Him all things are naked and open (Psalm 139:7-16). God's whole spirit being is present everywhere at the same time because He is infinite and is not bound by any limitations outside Himself.

All power is ascribed to God. He is omnipotent (Matthew 19:26; Revelation 19:6). In many ways the power of God has been demonstrated. He spoke and worlds came into being; He raised Christ from the dead; and He has done countless other things to display His infinite power.

All who have trusted the Lord Jesus Christ as Saviour have God as their heavenly Father. Such a thought is breathtaking. No greater privilege could ever be extended to anyone than to be a child of God. But as is the case with every privilege, there are corresponding responsibilities with being God's child.

It is an awesome thing to claim God as heavenly Father. And if the relationship is genuine, there will be evidence for it. There ought to be a resemblance between the Father and the son. Think for a moment about all the great characteristics of God. Our performance in life ought to correspond to these great perfections. We need not only to revel in these great truths, but also to reflect them in our lives.

For example, because God is self-existent, we ought to depend on Him for everything. Since He is infinite, we need to rest in His greatness as we approach the trials of life. He is holy, righteous and just; therefore holiness, uprightness and honesty should mark our lives. He is loving, merciful, and gracious, so we need to be the same in our lives and relations with others.

God is counting on us. He is depending on us to accurately represent Him on earth. We are indeed laborers together with Him. Don't disappoint Him.

Chapter Three
The Carpenter's Son?

Jesus of Nazareth is the most unique person who ever lived. During His life on earth the question, in one form or another, was often asked: "Who is this Jesus?" He asked the question Himself on one occasion of some of His fiercest critics. As the Pharisees were gathered around Him, He asked them plainly, "What think ye of Christ? whose son is he?" (Matthew 22:42).

The question is still being asked. And the answers, now as then, really stem from two views of Him. Either He is accepted for what He claimed to be, the very Son of God, or His claims are rejected and He is viewed as a mere man, a very God-like man, perhaps, but only a man nonetheless. If Jesus be accepted as only a man, we must go a step further in respect to His claims. If He knew He was not God but claimed to be anyway, He was a liar.

If He truly thought He was God but was sadly mistaken, He was mentally deranged. In other words, in the final analysis Christ was either a liar, a lunatic, or the Lord from glory.

I want you to see the Christ of Scripture in this study. Then, on the basis of what the Bible teaches about Jesus Christ, you must answer the question: What is my view of Christ?

Jesus' birth had nothing to do with His origin, for He lived before He was born. He has always existed. There never was a time when He was not. Of no one else born of woman is this true. Every human rightly traces his origin to his birth. But with Jesus that cannot be done.

Scripture clearly reveals that Jesus did not become the Son of God when He was born of Mary. He was always the Son. Jesus knew this, of course, and did not hesitate to talk about it to His earthly contemporaries. Said He, "I came out from God. I came forth from the Father, and am come into the world" (John 16:27,28). The Lord Jesus knew "neither beginning of days, nor end of life" (Hebrews 7:3). The Father loved the Son "before the foundation of the world" (John 17:24). Jesus prayed that His Father would glorify Him "with the glory which I had with thee before the world was" (verse 5).

No, the Son of God did not come into existence at His Birth. The Son was "given" (Isaiah 9:6). God so loved the world of mankind that He "gave" His only Son (John 3:16). Scripture is emphatic—Jesus lived eternally before He was born in time. He took on flesh and blood in time, but He is as eternal as is God the Father.

Jesus was born just as others are born. What was miraculous was His mother's conception. Mary became pregnant without having known a man (Luke 1:34); that is, without having had any sexual relations. An angel told Joseph not to fear to take Mary to be his wife because "that which is conceived in her is of the Holy Ghost" (Matthew 1:20).

Hundreds of years before the birth of Jesus God told the serpent, "I will put enmity between thee and the woman, and between thy seed and her seed" (Genesis 3:15). From this we see that Mary's miraculous conception, resulting in the virgin birth of Christ, was a vital part of early Old Testament prophecy. We might expect to read "his seed" referring to the male. But not so. The prophecy is clearly with respect to "her seed" and hers alone.

To Ahaz of old a divine sign was given: "A virgin shall conceive, and bear a son, and shall call his name Immanuel" (Isaiah 7:14). Then Matthew related this prophecy to the birth of Christ (Matthew 1:22,23).

Jesus claimed to be God. In fact, He said to His critics on one occasion, "If ye believe not that I am he, ye shall die in your sins" (John 8:24). "He that hath seen me hath seen the Father," He told Philip (John 14:9). "I am the bread of life," He claimed (John 6:35). He further stated: "I am the light of the world" (John 8:12); "I am the good shepherd" (John 10:11); and "I am the way, the truth, and the life" (John 14:6).

Scripture applies the very attributes or characteristics of God to Jesus Christ. Here are some examples: Christ, like God the Father, is immutable—He never changes, but is "the same yesterday, and to day and for ever" (Hebrews 13:8). All power belongs to Him, too. This is seen in that He upholds "all things by the word of his power" (Hebrews 1:3). And the Saviour knows all things. He knows the human heart (Matthew 15:19). He knew what was in man (John 2:25). The heart of Nathanael was fully known by Him (John 1:48). Furthermore, the holiness belonging only to God is His (Luke 1:35).

Jesus forgives sins as only God can do (Matthew 9:6,7); and He receives and welcomes worship due only to God (Matthew 2:11; 8:2).

Christ claimed absolute authority over the laws and institutions of God. He said He was greater than the temple and was Lord of the Sabbath (Matthew 12:6,8). He even claimed to be the object of saving faith along with the Father (John 17:3).

"I and my Father are one," said Jesus (John 10:30). Yet some modern-day critics still insist Jesus never really claimed to be God. But those who heard Him and opposed Him would disagree. They, in fact, said they were stoning Him not because of any good work He had done, but because He had made Himself equal with God (John 10:33). And they were right. He did claim to be equal with God, for He was and is God!

Even God, the Father, said of God, the Son, "Thy throne, O God, is forever and ever: a scepter of righteousness is the scepter of thy kingdom" (Hebrews 1:8). Yes, "God was manifest in the flesh" (I Timothy 3:16), and His name was the Lord Jesus Christ.

From the early history of the church to this very hour some stress Christ's humanity so much that they deny His deity. Others stress His deity to the point that they appear to deny His humanity. But the Bible is clear on this matter.

Jesus did not inherit any sin from Adam; He did not possess a nature or bent to sin; neither did He ever commit even so much as one sin. Although "without sin" (Hebrews 4:15), He was truly human.

Jesus was "manifest in the flesh" (I Timothy 3:16). He came in "the flesh" (I John 4:2). He was born of woman; thus He was fully human. As a man He grew and developed normally. He had a body, a soul and a spirit. Christ got weary as a man; He became hungry and thirsty. Sorrow gripped His heart as it does ours. He wept, too, and even got angry at those who desecrated the house of God (John 2:13-16).

The Son of God was the perfect Man. He showed to all mankind God's ideal of humanity and manhood. Without controversy, He is the Man, Christ Jesus. In Pilate's words, "Behold the man."

In *The Incomparable Christ,* J. Oswald Sanders relates a story about the great Daniel Webster who was once dining in Boston with some men of literary note. When the subject of Christ and Christianity came up, Webster did not hesitate to affirm his belief in both the deity and the humanity of Christ.

As the story goes, a Unitarian minister turned to Webster and asked, "Mr. Webster, can you comprehend how Jesus Christ could be both God and man?" Webster is said to have replied, "No, sir, I cannot understand it, and I would be ashamed to acknowledge Him as my Saviour if I could comprehend it. He could be no greater than myself, and such is my conviction of accountability to God, my sense of sinfulness before Him, and my knowledge of my own incapacity to recover myself, that I feel I need a superhuman Saviour."

Indeed we all need such a Saviour. And Jesus Christ meets the need for such a Saviour. In Him deity and humanity were joined in one person. He is the God-man. In the union He did not lose the identity of either His deity or His humanity.

Neither was there any lessening of either deity or humanity. Jesus Christ was totally God and totally man.

Christ spoke of Himself as one person. Never did the Saviour distinguish His divine person from His human person.

The rest of Scripture is also very clear on this. The Roman believers were told that God's Son, Jesus Christ our Lord, "was made of the seed of David according to the flesh; And declared to be the Son of God with power, according to the Spirit of holiness" (Romans 1:3,4). Paul also tells the Galatians, "God sent forth his Son, made of a woman" (Galatians 4:4). Again, the apostle presents the same truth to the Christians in Philippi. He clearly states that Christ Jesus was "equal with God" while being "made in the likeness of men" (Philippians 2:6,7). Surely no one can deny that Scripture plainly teaches the complete deity and the complete humanity of Jesus Christ.

Jesus' contemporaries had much to say about Him. His critics, the religious establishment, tried ever so hard to trap Him and to find some way to accuse Him. They asked Him on one occasion who He was. "I am who I said I was from the beginning—the Son of God," He told them. But they would not believe Him or receive Him. So He asked them, "Which of you convinceth me of sin?" (John 8:46). No one responded, for they had nothing to accuse Him of. They could not disprove His deity.

There were many, however, who truly believed Jesus Christ was God. Judas, Christ's betrayer, sorrowfully admitted he had betrayed innocent blood (Matthew 27:4). The centurion and others at the foot of the cross testified, "Truly this was the Son of God" (Matthew 27:54).

What about His friends, those closest to Him? What was their estimate of Him? John the Baptist declared that He was the "Lamb of God" (John 1:29). Nathanael exclaimed, "Thou art the Son of God" (John 1:49). The writer of the book of Hebrews said He was "without sin" (Hebrews 4:15). John the Apostle declared, "In him is no sin" (I John 3:5). Paul wrote, He "knew no sin" (II Corinthians 5:21).

But just because Jesus never sinned, that does not mean that He was untouched by temptation. The devil himself made an all-out effort to get Jesus to sin. The scene was in a wilderness, where Jesus had been fasting and praying for forty days and forty nights. At a time when Christ was physically weak, Satan came to Him to tempt Him (Matthew 4:1-11).

Satan made three attempts to get Jesus to do one thing—act independently of God. For that's what sin is—independence of God. First the tempter tantalized Jesus by telling Him to make bread out of stones to satisfy His hunger caused by the wilderness experience. Jesus refused. Next Satan tempted the Lord to jump from the highest point of the temple. He reasoned that when all the Jews gathered below saw how God would spare Christ they would then believe Him. Again Jesus refused to listen. Finally, Satan encouraged Christ to bow and worship him. Out there in the desert no one would see Christ do it. And Satan would give Him all the kingdoms of the world. But for the third time, Jesus refused to fall to Satan's temptations.

The Son of God countered each of Satan's attempts by quoting Scripture. Three times He said, "It is written." What a challenge that is to us! Our only source of victory over sin and Satan is the Word of God. Like Christ, we, too, must appeal to Scripture when temptation comes.

When Satan left Jesus, he left Him just as he had found Him—the sinless, spotless Lamb of God. That is why Christ can be our Saviour. And that is why He can give us victory, if we want it—because He was and still is without sin.

In His great condescension from Heaven to humanity the Son of God embraced a life in total dependence upon His Father. He became a man. True, He was more than a man; but He was man, nonetheless. Therefore He had needs. And so He prayed for these needs as well as for the needs of others. Jesus' life was indeed a life of prayer. He prayed for various needs, under varied circumstances. He prayed for Himself; He prayed for others.

In the beginning of His earthly pilgrimage and in His dying moments, Christ went to His Father in prayer.

Our Saviour's prayer life can be a tremendous encouragement. Sometimes we may be tempted to neglect prayer. "Doesn't God know what we need before we ask? Won't His will be worked out whether we pray or not?' And on and on go the questions. We don't know all the answers, because prayer is clothed in mystery. But we do know our Saviour prayed. And we know He exhorted us to pray. Therefore I pray and I will continue to pray. Will you?

You cannot be neutral when it comes to Jesus Christ. You must decide to be for Him or against Him. There simply is no middle ground.

Proud Pontious Pilate turned a corner in his life one day and came face to face with Jesus Christ. History reports that Jesus was on trial before Pilate. But in reality it was the other way around—Pilate was on trial before Jesus. "What shall I do then with Jesus which is called Christ?" Pilate asked the angry mob (Matthew 27:22). He had to make a decision.

But the Roman governor was not the only one who must ponder that question. Everyone must. Have you considered what you will do with Jesus Christ?

Chapter Four
It Is Finished!

"A woman's work is never done." Men have been reminded of this again and again, sometimes with more force than at other times. And there is much truth to this maxim. The fact is, neither women nor men ever really have all their work completely finished. We try to keep up, to get by, but there is always more to do.

But Jesus Christ was different. He completely finished the work He came to earth to do. While on the cross, He uttered the word *tetelestai*—"It is finished." But what was it that was finished at that moment? Why should the Saviour make such an announcement? Was He telling the people His life was ended?

Yes, Christ's earthly life was finished. He was about to dismiss His spirit, to die physically. He would have no more suffering, so that, too, was finished. But is that all that was finished? To what did our Lord refer when He uttered that single word, *tetelestai?*

I believe the Saviour meant the provision of salvation which He had come to make was finished. His hour had come—the hour established in eternity past—when full and final atonement was to be made for sin. The divine work of redemption was completed. The Father would demand no more. All the demands of divine justice were fully satisfied. The price was paid. Nothing more could be done to make sinners savable. Christ had paid it all!

From the purely human point of view Christ died because He was put to death by being crucified. The Jewish leaders had succeeded in having Christ arraigned before the Roman authorities. They also incited the people against Him. The result was that He experienced the most cruel, humiliating form of death known to man—crucifixion.

But what was the divine purpose for Christ's death? Why did God the Father allow men to treat His Son this way? That is what we want to know.

Some would have us believe the purpose of God the Father in the death of His Son was to obtain redemption and forgiveness of sins for all men by supplying all with sufficient grace to believe if they will. This view seems to place all the responsibility upon man to believe, to respond favorably to the grace extended to him. This view does not take seriously enough the Bible's teaching of the total inability of man to respond apart from the Spirit's work in his heart.

Others insist Christ died to redeem only the elect, those chosen in Him before the foundation of the world (Ephesians 1:4). For these people, Christ's death did not simply make all men savable. Instead His death actually secured the salvation only of those who will believe—it saves them. In other words, according to this view, the cross of Christ secures and applies its own benefits.

But, there is still another response given to the question, Why did Christ die? This answer appears to satisfy the total Scriptural presentation better than either of the other two explanations. In brief, the view is that Christ died in order to make possible the salvation of all men, and to make certain the salvation of those who trust Him alone as Saviour. Why did Christ die? He died to make provision of salvation for all. That is the abundant and repeated testimony of Scripture. In addition to such vital passages as Romans 5; II Corinthians 5; II Peter 2:1 and I John 2:1,2, we could cite every "all" and each "whosoever" of the New Testament. Yes, Christ died for every man. But the finished work of Christ must be appropriated. There are literally dozens of times in Scripture when the individual is called upon to receive, to believe, to trust in order that God's gracious provision of salvation be made personal.

No, Christ did not die to save all men. If He did He is defeated, because all are not saved. He did die, though, to make salvation possible for all. He died because He loved the world (John 3:16). God is not willing that *any* should perish (II Peter 3:9).

There is hardly a more important question than, "For whom did Christ die?" We want to know, we *must* know, who is included in the substitution Christ made at Calvary nearly two thousand years ago.

If we believe Scripture teaches that Christ died to provide salvation for all, we have the answer to our question. For if this is the case, obviously He died for every member of Adam's race. If, on the other hand, we believe Christ died only for those who will be saved, we have a very different answer to the question now before us.

What does the Bible say about this all important question? In some places Scripture states very clearly that Christ died for those who will be saved. Jesus Himself said He would lay down His life for the sheep (John 10:15). Speaking of fellow believers, Paul said, "Christ hath redeemed us" (Galatians 3:13). Again the apostle said, "Christ loved the church, and gave himself for it" (Ephesians 5:25). It is the "church of God" which Christ "purchased with his own blood" (Acts 20:28).

On the other hand, in many other passages of Scripture we are told that Christ died for the world of men. "Behold the Lamb of God, which taketh away the sin of the world" (John 1:29). "To wit, that God was in Christ, reconciling the world unto himself" (II Corinthians 5:19). "The Father sent the Son to be the Saviour of the world" (I John 4:14).

The word "whosoever" is used over 100 times in the New Testament with respect to Christ's death and man's need to respond to it (see John 3:16; Acts 2:21; Romans 10:13).

Without any attempt to distinguish kinds of people Scripture declares the Saviour came to seek and save the "lost" (Luke 19:10). Christ died for the "ungodly" (Romans 5:6). He gave Himself a ransom for "all" (I Timothy 2:6). He tasted death for "every man" (Hebrews 2:9).

So we have seen that in some passages, the Bible presents Christ as dying for select groups. In other passages, we read that He died for all men. What are we to do, then, with the Biblical testimony on this matter? Is there a contradiction in the Bible? No, not at all. Both of these Biblical emphases present a harmonious truth.

If we base our answer to the question "For whom did Christ die?" on the Scripture which limits His death to being for a select group, we will have trouble with all the Scripture which broadens the scope of His death. If, on the other hand, we base our view on the many passages which speak of His death as being for all, we will have no difficulty with those Scriptures which speak of it as being only for some. In other words, the Scriptures which state Christ died for some are easily harmonized with those that say He died for all, because nowhere are we told He died *only* for some.

The accomplishments of the Saviour through His death were many. But unless we see Christ's death as the means by which He gave Himself as the substitute for sinners, we have completely missed its meaning. Christ died in my place; He died instead of me. True, He died for my benefit; but more than that, He paid for my sin so that I need not pay for it. In fact, I *could not* have paid for my sin. That is why Christ paid for it instead. He died as my substitute. He said of Himself, "The Son of man came . . . to give his life a ransom for many" (Matthew 20:28). Jesus was stressing, in the strongest possible language, the substitutionary nature of His death.

Paul reminds us that God "made him to be sin for us, who [Christ] knew no sin" (II Corinthians 5:21). Another apostle put it this way: He "bare our sins in his own body on the tree" (I Peter 2:24).

This means that all of God's wrath toward sin was poured out upon His Son.

Christ bore it all. All the sin of all men of all ages was heaped on Him. The Father's judgment upon sin fell on the Son. His substitution for sin, His death in the sinner's place, is the one accomplishment which is basic to everything else which was done that day.

Because Christ took our place on Calvary, He is able to provide us with three things: redemption, reconciliation and propitiation. At first glance these words appear difficult to understand. But they really are not difficult at all. Let's look at each of them more closely to see how they are used in the New Testament.

Redemption has a special relation to sin. It refers to the fact that the price demanded by God for our sin has been paid by Christ. He has redeemed us.

Three basic words translated "redeem" are used in the New Testament. One of them gives the idea of purchasing something, paying the price for it (II Peter 2:1). Another carries with it the idea not only of paying the purchase price, but also of removing the item from the place of sale (Galatians 4:4,5). Finally, a third word emphasizes the release of someone for a ransom. It has a special reference to the purchase of slaves (I Peter 1:18-20).

Change is, of necessity, involved in *reconciliation.* To be made compatible with, to be changed from enmity to friendship, is to be reconciled. Man, of course, is the one who needs to be changed in order to be fitted for Heaven. God does not change; He *cannot* change (Malachi 3:6). When He saves a believing sinner He does not do so because He decides to change His attitude toward sin and become lenient. No, God still hates sin. But through the substitutionary death of His Son God made it possible to save man. He made man savable by accepting the sacrifice of His Son for man's sin (Romans 5:6-11; II Corinthians 5:17-19).

Propitiation is perhaps the least understood of the three words under discussion. The word "propitiate" means simply "to satisfy" (I John 2:1,2). But who has been satisfied? Who alone needs to be satisfied? God! His holiness and hatred of sin demanded that He be satisfied before man could ever enter His presence. It was through Christ's blood shed on the cross that God was satisfied (Romans 3:25).

All three of these great provisions are available to every member of Adam's lost race. However, if they are to benefit the individual, they must be appropriated by faith. The provisions have been made. The work is finished. But only when they are claimed by faith in Christ who made them are they applied to the individual's account. No one is redeemed, no one is reconciled to God, no one benefits from the satisfaction Christ made until he trusts Christ as His own Saviour. Then and only then do the universal provisions become individualized.

Believers often forget the significance of the finished work of Christ for us. He who redeemed us by His blood is our only plea. The completed work of Christ is the ground, the basis, for our continued forgiveness and cleansing (I John 1:5—2:2). Cleansing from the defilements of sin is provided by the same Saviour whom we trusted in the first place for our salvation.

No longer do we need to be slaves to the drive to sin within us. That old drive and desire is still with us, but it has been rendered inoperative. Its binding force and fetters have been broken. In the power of Christ we can say "no" to sin, because all who are in Christ have died to sin (Romans 6:6). This means the victory Christ achieved at the cross over sin and Satan and all the demons of Hell belongs to each and every child of God.

Very often we forget about the present ministry of Christ. We give so much attention to what He did in the past and what we believe He will do in the future that we bypass His present ministry. Without neglecting or minimizing either our Lord's past or future work, we do need to know about what He is doing for us now.

At the Father's right hand Christ lives to make intercession for His own (Hebrews 7:25). He is our great High Priest. But contrary to the Old Testament priesthood and every form of human priesthood, Christ's priesthood is eternal and unchangeable (Hebrews 7:3,24).

When Christ died the veil of the temple was torn from top to bottom (Matthew 27:51). This unusual phenomenon was indicative of Christ's finished work and the open access through Him to the Father. Now all who trust Him alone as Saviour are priests and have direct access to the very throne of God. Believers in this age do not *have* a priest, as they did before Christ's death. All believers today *are* priests (I Peter 2:9). And Christ is our High Priest—our intercessor.

In addition to being intercessor, Christ is the "advocate" of all who know Him as Saviour (I John 2:1). That is, He represents His own before the throne of God.

Intercession relates to Christ's work toward the believer, with a view of preventing sin in the believer's life. We were included in Christ's great prayer of intercession before His death (John 17). And there is every reason to believe He continues that ministry for us today. Advocacy, on the other hand, relates primarily to Christ's work after we fall into sin. Then it is He who pleads our case, not by claiming innocence for us, but by presenting us before the Father, clothed in His righteousness and under His redemptive care.

All that Christ is doing now is based upon what He did in His death. At the cross He offered Himself as the full and final sacrifice for sin. Now, on the basis of that finished and acceptable sacrifice, Christ administers its benefits to those who belong to Him.

No one needs to add anything or even *can* add anything to the redemption God offers men. Christ, the Son of God, made full atonement. God the Father is fully satisfied with the finished work of His Son. We know this because He raised Him from the dead.

But there is some work that remains to be done. And this task is ours. God has charged each of His own, you and me, to be His ambassadors. As we share the Word of God, the Spirit of God will draw men and women, boys and girls to Himself.

Our witness for Christ does not add anything to the finished work at Calvary. Not even does the individual's faith in Christ add anything. There is nothing to add. The work is finished.

But God wants us to tell others about the finished work. This is our task. Angels have not been told to do it. We have. This is God's method. To us He has committed the task of spreading the good news. And *that* task remains unfinished.

Chapter Five
The Third Person

We Christians do not serve three Gods. We are not tritheists. We are monotheists, serving one God. Our God is one in essence, yet three in subsistence. That is, He has manifested Himself in three personal distinctions. God, the Father, is the first Person of the Godhead. God, the Son, is the second Person. God, the Holy Spirit, is the third Person. Three distinct and divine persons make up the holy Trinity; yet mystery of mysteries, God remains one.

The Holy Spirit is perhaps the least understood member of the Trinity. Until recent years much more was said in churches and in religious literature about the Father and the Son than about the Holy Spirit. However, with the rise of the charismatic movement, this picture has changed. Today there is much more being said about the Holy Spirit, especially about His work, than there was even just a few years ago.

The contemporary interest in the Holy Spirit is sufficient cause to reexamine Scripture to see what we are to believe about the third Person of the Trinity. It seems that people either neglect or overemphasize the person and the work of the Holy Spirit. God spare us from both extremes! If the work of God is to prosper in our lives and in our churches, the Holy Spirit of God must be given His rightful place.

People frequently refer to the third Person of the Trinity as "it." This reflects the view that the Spirit is merely a power or an influence in the world. Of course, not everyone who speaks of the Holy Spirit in this way means to deny His personality. Sometimes the expression simply reflects an unfortunate choice of words, without any intention of being disrespectful. However, for others who actually do not believe the Spirit is a person, the choice of words is intentional.

Why should we believe the Holy Spirit of God is a person? Is there Biblical grounds for such a belief? The answer is an emphatic "yes!" Four particular emphases in the Bible substantiate this conviction.

First, what the Spirit possesses convinces us that He is, indeed, a person. To the Spirit belong all the elements essential to personality. An "it"—a power, force, or influence—does not possess intellect. Yet the Spirit, we are told, has a "mind" (Romans 8:27).

Mere powers don't have feelings, either. But the Spirit does. He is grieved or hurt every time we sin (Ephesians 4:30). He loves, too (Romans 15:30), and provides love for God's children (II Timothy 1:7).

Self-determination or will is also characteristic of the Spirit. When He gives us gifts or abilities to use in service for the Lord, He does so according to His own will (I Corinthians 12:11). All these characteristics definitely indicate the presence of a personality.

Second, what the third Person of the Godhead performs assures us He is not just an "it." Can an "it" teach? Hardly. Only persons are able to teach. And the Holy Spirit teaches in fulfillment of Christ's promise (John 14:26). He testifies, too, and bears witness or gives confirmation (Romans 8:16). Leading the believer is also one of the Spirit's works (Romans 8:14). And on at least one occasion the Spirit said He had called men into special service for God (Acts 13:2). Actions such as these can be performed only by a person.

Third, in the Bible we are told the Holy Spirit gains responses which could be given only to a person. For example, people either obey or disobey Him (Acts 10:19-21). Ananias lied to Him (Acts 5:3). Men either resist Him or reverence Him (Acts 7:51; Psalm 51:11).

Fourth, the third Person of the Trinity is presented in Scripture in such a way that to deny His personality is to deny the truthfulness of the Bible. The men who recorded Scripture repeatedly used personal pronouns to refer to the Holy Spirit. They even used certain kinds of personal pronouns when, according to every normal rule of Greek grammar, we would not expect them to appear.

For instance, the Greek word for spirit is *pneuma.* It is neuter in gender, neither masculine nor feminine. Normally, whenever a pronoun is used in the place of a noun, it should agree in gender—in this case it should be neuter. However, according to *The Holy Spirit* by Charles C. Ryrie, "in several places the biblical writers did not follow this normal procedure of grammar, and instead of using a neuter pronoun in place of the neuter noun *pneuma,* they deliberately contradicted the grammatical rule and used masculine pronouns. . . .This shows they considered the Spirit to be a person and not merely a thing."

We know the Holy Spirit is God because in Scripture the attributes or characteristics of God are applied to Him. He is seen as performing works only God can do. But most importantly, Scripture actually refers to the Holy Spirit as God.

First, let's look at a few of the attributes of God which the Spirit is said to possess. The psalmist indicated that the Spirit is omnipresent: "Whither shall I go from thy spirit? or whither shall I flee from thy presence?" (Psalm 139:7). This rhetorical question implies the answer, "nowhere."

Just as God the Father and God the Son know all things, so does the Spirit of God. He is, in fact, the Spirit of wisdom (Ephesians 1:17). "The Spirit searcheth all things, yea, the deep things of God. For what man knoweth the things of a man, save the spirit of man which is in him? even so the things of God knoweth no man, but the Spirit of God" (I Corinthians 2:10,11).

All power belongs to God alone. And by His great works the Holy Spirit demonstrates that He possesses omnipotence—all power. Job testified to this effect when he said the Spirit of God made him and gave him life (Job 33:4).

Next we can find support for the deity of the Spirit by looking at the works which the Bible says he performed and continues to perform. In the very opening verses of Genesis we are told of the Spirit's part in the creation of the world and of man (Genesis 1:2). The third Person of the Godhead was also responsible for the conception of the Christ child in Mary's womb (Luke 1:35). When you trusted Christ as your personal Saviour you were born again. The new birth is the Spirit's work of giving life to the spiritually dead sinner (John 3:6). How could the Spirit have performed these miracles if He is not God?

Does Scripture ever actually refer to the third Person of the Trinity, the Holy Spirit, as God? Yes, it does. One outstanding passage is Acts 5.

In the early days of the church some of the Christians volunteered to sell their possessions and pool their resources so that they could help those in special need. A man named Ananias and his wife Saphira apparently wanted to look good before the others in the church (that sounds rather contemporary, doesn't it?). So these two sold some property and pretended to bring all the proceeds to the leaders of the church. But they lied about the amount, for they had kept back part of it. Peter rebuked them, and they met with a tragic death because they lied "to the Holy Ghost, . . . unto God" (Acts 5:3,4).

The fact that the Holy Spirit is one with the other Persons of the Trinity is clearly revealed when He is called the Spirit of the Father (Matthew 10:20) and the Spirit of the Son (Galatians 4:6). These titles underscore the unity in the Godhead. All three members cooperate and concur with each other in their work.

The many references to the third Person as "the Spirit" express not only His deity, since "God is a Spirit" (John 4:24), but they also indicate how He manifests Himself in the world. Jesus told Nicodemus that even as a person can hear the wind but not tell where it is, "so is every one that is born of the Spirit" (John 3:8).

It is generally accepted that absolute holiness belongs to God alone. And yet the third Person of the Trinity is referred to as "the Holy Spirit" more frequently than any other name. In Psalm 143:10 David said to God, "Thy Spirit is good." And yet we know "there is none good but one, that is, God" (Matthew 19:17). Again, the Holy Spirit's deity is firmly established by inspired Scripture.

We are told in Hebrews 9:14 that the Holy Spirit is eternal. He is as eternal as God is, because He is God. Once more, Scripture confirms His deity.

In His parting words to His disciples Jesus spoke of the Spirit, whom He and the Father would send, as "the Comforter" (John 14:16,26; 15:26; 16:7). Perhaps the best English translation of the Greek word Christ used in these passages would be "friend." The Holy Spirit was sent into the world to be the divine Friend of God's people. Isn't that terrific? He came to perform other ministries with respect to the unregenerate, but for the believer He came as a friend. How revealing this designation is! It speaks of the Spirit's interest in and intimacy with God and His people. It also further establishes His deity since He is another of the same kind as Jesus. And it establishes His personality, too, because powers and influences can't be friends.

Maybe you have been wondering as you read, "What difference does it make whether I believe in the personality and deity of the Holy Spirit or not?" First of all, since the Bible speaks so clearly on these matters, we really have no choice but to believe them. That is, we have no choice if we would honor the God who inspired Scripture. True, we cannot comprehend it all. We have many unanswered questions. And yet our inability to understand must not cause us to doubt God. For no one can experience peace with God if he refuses to believe what God has said.

Isn't it awesome to think that everyone, believers and unbelievers alike, has to meet up with the Person of God, the Holy Spirit? That is a highly important aspect of this matter of the Holy Spirit's relationship to us. When the Spirit is spurned, either by a believer or by one who refuses to place his trust in Christ, the very God of the Bible is being disregarded. The One being neglected is not a mighty power or force, not an "it", but the Person of God, who is at work in our world and in our lives.

As believers, let us honor the third Person of the Godhead. Let us love Him and trust Him to use us as He effects God's will upon this earth.

Chapter Six
The Third Person at Work

Charismatic. Speaking in tongues. Slain in the Spirit. Divine healing. Baptism of the Spirit. The fullness of the Spirit. These and other similar expressions are becoming more and more popular. In the church and outside it the Holy Spirit, especially His work, is the subject of much discussion.

Why is it that believers, and even many unbelievers, talk more about the Holy Spirit today than they did just a few years ago? Or more importantly, why has the charismatic movement become so popular and spread so widely in our day?

Whatever the reason may be for the present state of affairs, it is high time for us to get the Biblical perspective on the Holy Spirit and His work.

It is commonly thought that God, the Father, was alone responsible for the creation of all things. Unfortunately, both the Son and the Spirit are often slighted when it comes to a discussion of origins.

But the truth is, the Bible ascribes the work of creation to God as an entity. Scripture does not always distinguish which member of the Godhead is involved. And yet there are instances where both the Son and the Spirit are specifically mentioned as agents in creation.

For example, Moses wrote, "The Spirit of God moved upon the face of the waters" (Genesis 1:2). "By his spirit," Job declared, God "hath garnished the heavens" (Job 26:13). Job also confessed, "The Spirit of God hath made me, and the breath of the Almighty hath given me life" (Job 33:4).

In addition to the specific statements of Scripture, we have warrant for saying the Holy Spirit had a vital part in creation because of His relationship to the Father and the Son.

Through the Holy Spirit God revealed exactly what He wanted the human penmen to record. As Peter said, the men who wrote Scripture were "moved by the Holy Ghost" (II Peter 1:21). Many, many times the prophets were bold to say, "The Spirit of the Lord spake by me" (II Samuel 23:2) or something very similar. Ezekiel's prophecy contains a number of such expressions (Ezekiel 2:2; 8:3; 11:1,24). Likewise the New Testament bears the same testimony (Acts 1:16; Hebrews 3:7).

It is true, as many people emphasize, that on the day of Pentecost the Holy Spirit came with new and special ministries. But He was also very active before that significant day. The Saviour told Nicodemus of the Spirit's work of regeneration—giving life (John 3:3-7). And we may safely assume from this New Testament teaching that the Spirit is the one who imparted life from the beginning. He is the life-giver.

It is also apparent from the Old Testament that the Holy Spirit indwelt at least some believers. In the New Testament it is clearly taught that the Spirit permanently indwells every child of God. This does not seem to have been true of everyone in the Old Testament who was rightly related to God. But it is clear that the Spirit did indwell some (Numbers 27:18; Daniel 4:8).

Many of those who labored for God in special ministries were indwelt by the Spirit of God (Exodus 28:3; 31:1; Numbers 11:17). The Holy Spirit is said to be *in* certain individuals (Genesis 41: 38), *upon* others (Judges 3:10), and even to have *filled* some (Exodus 31:3).

The Holy Spirit's pre-Pentecost ministry in the life of Christ was especially important. At Christmastime we all think of the Christ child. And that is the way it should be. And yet the part the Holy Spirit played in the birth, life, and death of Christ must not be neglected. The Christ child was conceived in the womb of the virgin Mary by a sovereign work of the Holy Spirit (Matthew 1:20; Luke

1:35). The Saviour's public life began when He was anointed by the Holy Spirit (Luke 4:18). And throughout Christ's entire life and ministry the Spirit ministered to Him and through Him.

The work of creation was finished on the sixth day. The Spirit's work of revelation and inspiration has also ceased. And the Spirit's ministry in the life of Christ has long been complete. But by no means is the Holy Spirit idle. He daily performs ministries in and toward believers as well as toward unbelievers.

Eternal life is the result of the work of the Holy Spirit (Titus 3:5). This gift comes at the time of faith in Christ; and that faith comes as a result of the conviction of the Spirit (John 16:7-11).

At the time of the new birth each believing sinner is spiritually placed into the body of Christ, united with all who have trusted in Him since the birthday of the church—the day of Pentecost (I Corinthians 12:12,13). Also, all who trust Christ alone for salvation are spiritually united with Christ, who is the Head of His body, the church (Romans 6:1-5). This uniting of the believer with Christ and other believers is brought about by the baptism of the Spirit. The Spirit is the One who baptizes or identifies each believer, at the time of salvation, with Christ and with every other believer. All who are in the body have been baptized by the Spirit.

Many people have the tendency to refer to a building where worship services are held as "the house of God." But God does not dwell in temples made with hands. The body of the child of God is the dwelling place of the Holy Spirit. And a person doesn't have to be a spiritual giant to be indwelt by the Holy Spirit. To the Corinthians, who were perhaps the most carnal of the early Christians, Paul wrote, "Know ye not that your body is the temple of the Holy Ghost which is in you, which ye have of God, and ye are not your own?" (I Corinthians 6:19). What a gift believers have—the Holy Spirit! (Romans 5:5; I Corinthians 2:2). He who does not have the Spirit is not God's child (Romans 8:9).

When the Holy Spirit indwells a person, He is with him forever (John 14:27). The Spirit is always there to assist us, to convict us, and to comfort us. We are never truly alone. The next time you begin to think you are alone, remember God's promise to you. Remember His Spirit's presence the next time your world crashes in on you.

Thank God for security in Christ! At the moment of salvation each and every believer, regardless of his age, his background, or his knowledge, is sealed by the Spirit (Ephesians 4:30). And the Holy Spirit is not only the sealer, but He is also the seal. This seal identifies us as God's possession. We belong to Him. And the seal is also the "earnest," the pledge, of our inheritance. The Spirit's presence in us is the assurance from God that we will receive all that has been promised to us.

Nowhere in the Bible is anyone ever exhorted to be baptized by the Spirit. This is because the work of Spirit baptism is completed at the moment of faith in Christ. But believers *are* exhorted to be *filled* with the Spirit (Ephesians 5:18).

To be filled with the Spirit does not mean to get more of the Spirit. It means, rather, to allow the Spirit to have more of us. When Paul told the Ephesian believers to be filled with the Spirit, he compared this filling to being drunk with wine (Ephesians 5:18). And in two other places in the New Testament, the infilling of the Spirit is associated with the effects of strong drink (Luke 1:15; Acts 2:4-15). One who is drunk is under the control of alcohol. One who is filled with the Spirit is under the control of the Spirit.

It is important to note, too, that being filled with the Spirit is an experience which can be repeated. We know this because of what Paul told the Ephesians about it. He used the present tense and the imperative mood of the Greek verb, which refers to a command for *continuous* action.

Since we are commanded to be filled with the Spirit, we must have some part in the filling. In order to be filled with the Holy Spirit, the believer must cooperate with Him by responding to His invitation. And how do we do this? The word "obedience" says it all. We are filled, or controlled, by the Spirit when we obey the Word of God.

In three different places in the New Testament we are given lists of these gifts, these abilities for service (I Corinthians 12; Romans 12; Ephesians 4). Doubtlessly there are other divinely given abilities for service but these lists include the crucial ones. The Holy Spirit bestows these gifts "for the perfecting of the saints" (Ephesians 4:12). The word translated "perfecting" means "equipping" or "fitting." By the exercise of the gift or gifts God has given, each one in the body of Christ grows and functions to His glory.

Some of the gifts of the Spirit were particularly and exclusively related to the days of the apostles. The gift of apostleship, for example, ceased when the Apostle John died.

Prophecy was another gift of the Spirit. Is it operative now? No, because the canon of Scripture is complete. All the revelation God wants us to have has been given, in the form of His written Word.

The New Testament gift of speaking in tongues is much debated these days. Some argue vehemently that it is still operative. Others argue just as vehemently that it is not.

Several things lend strong support to the view that the gift of tongues ceased when the New Testament was completed.

First, speaking in tongues (using a language that hasn't been studied) was a sign gift. Paul described the gift this way in his instruction to people who were misusing it (I Corinthians 14:22). He further declared that speaking in tongues was a sign to the nation Israel (verse 21; cf. Isaiah 28:11,12). In other words, to verify themselves and the message they proclaimed to the Jews, the apostles were given the ability to speak in a language they had not studied. Since the nation Israel has been set aside temporarily because of unbelief, and since Scripture is complete and a verifying sign is not needed, we conclude that the gift of tongues has ceased.

Second, every instance of the exercise of the gift of tongues in the New Testament was in association with an apostle. Since the gift of apostleship has ceased, it follows that the accompanying gift of speaking in tongues has also ceased.

Third, Scripture states emphatically that tongues would cease (I Corinthians 13:8).

Fourth, second-generation Christians were told that sign gifts, which included tongues, had already ceased (Hebrews 2:3,4). They had served their purpose in "confirming" the apostles' oral testimony concerning "so great salvation."

The Bible does not say a great deal about the work of the Holy Spirit after the return of the Lord for His own. But we do know that He will continue to restrain sin until the church is raptured. Until the rapture the Spirit will "hinder"—hold back—the full onslaught of wickedness (II Thessalonians 2:6,7).

Since many will be brought to faith in Christ during the future Great Tribulation period (Revelation 7:9-14; 14:1-5) we may assume that the Spirit will perform the work of regeneration during that time. We can also assume that the Holy Spirit will indwell Tribulation saints, seal them, fill them, and help them to understand God's Word, just as He does today. But there is one ministry the Spirit now performs that He will not perform after Christ's return for His church. He will no longer baptize believers, because the church formed by this baptism will have been raptured before the Tribulation begins.

During the future millennial reign of Christ, when He will rule from David's throne in Jerusalem for 1000 years, the Holy Spirit will be very active. He will be poured out upon the redeemed of that period in an unprecedented and unrestrained way (Joel 2:28). Christ Himself will exercise His functions in the power of the Spirit (Isaiah 11:1-5; 42:1-4). Universal peace and righteousness will prevail on the earth (Isaiah 32:15; Romans 14:17). What man now strives for, God will finally bring to pass.

There ought to be a harmonious relationship between the child of God and the Spirit of God. And this harmony should be obvious from our behavior. Scripture gives two basic positive commands and two basic negative commands regarding the response of each believer to the work of the Holy Spirit.

Let's look at the positive commands first. We have already looked at one of these—"Be filled with the Spirit" (Ephesians 5:18). As we have seen, this calls for obedience to Scripture and submission to God. Every child of God is also told to "walk in the Spirit" (Galatians 5:16). Stated simply, this means we are to live in dependence upon the Holy Spirit on a day by day, moment by moment basis. When we walk, each step we take is dependent upon the one already taken. And in the Christian life we are to walk, or live, by depending upon the Holy Spirit. He provides the enablement and encouragement we need.

The negative commands given to believers with regard to the Holy Spirit are "Quench not the Spirit" (I Thessalonians 5:19), and "Grieve not the Spirit" (Ephesians 4:30). We quench the Spirit when we say "no" to Him, when we resist Him, when we disobey God's Word. We grieve the Spirit when we sin. Sin in a believer's life hurts the Spirit and, of course, hinders His work in us and through us.

Chapter Seven
Spirit Beings! Really?

Not too long ago you very likely would have been laughed at if you said you believed Satan and angels actually existed. Intelligent people were not supposed to believe in them. But today it's different. Through all the news media, religious and secular, we are being confronted with reams of information about the spirit world.

The emphasis today seems to be upon wicked spirits and Satan—the occult—rather than upon holy angels. The word *occult* comes from the Latin word *occultus* which means "hidden, dark, mysterious, secret." It has come to be used to describe the phenomena which go beyond, or at least seem to go beyond, our world of the five senses. Authorities claim that at least ten million Americans dabble in occult arts—witchcraft, magic, Black Masses, blood-drinking orgies, the crystal ball, astrology, horoscopes, and even the Ouija Board. There are Satanic churches where people actually worship Satan. In 1966 Anton La Vey founded the First Church of Satan in San Francisco. Today he claims to have a membership of over 10,000. You can browse through almost any bookstore and find a large number of titles dealing with almost any aspect of the occult imaginable. And more and more films like *Rosemary's Baby* and *The Exorcist* are being produced.

"Why the new interest in the spirit world?" you might ask. "Have masses of people finally come to believe the Bible and its emphasis upon the reality of Satan and demons?" That hardly seems to be the case. I believe, instead, that the widespread interest in Satan stems from neglect, on the part of some, and rejection, on the part of others, of God's Word. For centuries men have tried to replace that inspired authority with countless numbers of things, all of which have sadly failed. And man is still hungry, reaching out for reality. So many are turning to the world of the occult in a vain attempt to fill the vacuum created by rejecting God's truth.

Not all interest in the spirit world is evil, for not all spirits are evil. Yes, holy angels do exist. They are personal realities, having been created by God. Over half of the sixty-six books of the Bible not only refer to angels but also give information about them. Christ taught quite extensively about angels, as we read in the Gospels. And we must make a choice with respect to what He said about these heavenly beings. We must believe either that He told the truth, or that He told falsehoods, or that He was misinformed about the subject. We must decide. And all those who believe the Bible to be God's Word and who know Christ as Saviour realize He always speaks the truth, for He *is* truth (John 14:6).

We are not told in Scripture when the angels were created. But since they sang together and shouted for joy when God placed the foundations of the earth in order (Job 38:4,7), it stands to reason that they were created before the creation of the world.

Nothing sinful ever came from God's creative hand, therefore we know the angels were made perfect. But they all had what we might call a probation period, a time of testing. Some of them sinned when Satan did. Those who sinned were confirmed in their wickedness and those who did not were confirmed in their holiness.

Growing older is no problem among angels. They are all the same age. They do not die (Luke 20:36); neither do they reproduce (Matthew 22:28-30).

There is evidently some organization among the holy angels. While all worship God and serve Him, some have special responsibilities. The angel Michael is called "one of the chief princes" (Daniel 10:13). Gabriel had the unique privilege of announcing the conception of Christ to the virgin Mary (Luke 1:26-35). And others are said to have special tasks, presiding over "principalities and powers" (Ephesians 3:10).

Angels possess the marks of personality. Their intelligence is evident throughout Scripture. They desire to understand salvation, since they have never experienced sin or redemption (I Peter 1:12). Holy angels rejoice in the presence of God (Luke 15:10). They worship God (Hebrews 1:6). Some of them are said to have exercised unusual power on some occasions. They all "excel in strength" (Psalm 103:20). And one of their number even rolled the stone away from Christ's tomb (Matthew 28:2). In the future some will exert control over certain elements of nature (Revelation 7:1; 14:18).

Holy angels today observe human affairs. As we have already seen, they have an intense desire to look into our salvation (I Peter 1:10-12). Paul told the women in Corinth to keep their heads covered because the angels were watching them (I Corinthians 11:10). He had already told the Corinthian believers that they were made a spectacle unto the angels (I Corinthians 4:9). And he charged Timothy before God, Christ, and the elect angels to conduct himself wisely as a faithful minister (I Timothy 5:21).

In every major aspect of our Lord's life, He was accompanied by holy angels. Beginning with His birth, through His life of ministry, in His death and resurrection, and even in His promised return, we are told of the involvement of holy angels with the Saviour.

Holy angels minister for God in our behalf (Hebrews 1:14). The Bible records many instances when these spirit beings assisted the people of God. And I believe that they still work for us in mysterious, though invisible, ways. But we are not to worship angels. God alone is to be worshiped. Even the angels themselves request that man not bow down to them in worship (Revelation 22:9).

The Bible ascribes a number of names to the archenemy of God. Each one is descriptive of him and his work. Over fifty times he is called *Satan,* characterizing him as the resister or adversary. *Devil* means he is a slanderer of God to man and man to God. *Beelzebub* makes him the prince of demons; *serpent* reflects his beguiling nature; *tempter* describes his work.

Paul called Satan the "god of this world" (II Corinthians 4:4), the prince of the power of the air," and "the spirit that now worketh in the children of disobedience" (Ephesians 2:2). John said he deceives the whole world (Revelation 12:9) and accuses the brethren (verse 10).

Satan was not created wicked. Like the angels, he was perfect when he came from God's hand. Before his fall Satan had a unique position of responsibility among the holy angels and before Jehovah-God. Great privileges were his (Ezekiel 28:11-15). But sin was found in him (verse 15). Five terrible "I wills" characterized his awful sin (Isaiah 14:13,14). He had pride and a desire to be independent of God, his creator. Isn't that at the heart of all sin?

Six time periods mark Satan's career. First, there was the time from his creation to the time of his fall. Second is the period since his fall, in which he has been and continues to be "seeking whom he may devour" (I Peter 5:8). Third, during the future Tribulation period Satan will be unusually active, especially during the last three and one half years of that period. Fourth, after the Tribulation described in Revelation 6—19 Satan will be confined in the abyss during the 1000-year reign of Christ (Revelation 20:1-3). Fifth, at the end of the 1000 years he will be loosed for a little season (verses 3,7). Finally, Satan will be cast into the Lake of Fire where he and all the Christ-rejectors of all ages will "be tormented day and night for ever and ever" (Revelation 20:10).

Satan is presently busily engaged in his evil work. He is active twenty-four hours a day, sixty minutes an hour. The word "counterfeit" thoroughly describes Satan's work. Through unbelievers in religious circles, he mimics God and His work (II Corinthians 11:13-15).

As you might expect, Satan blinds the thought processes of those who do not believe in Christ so as to keep them from believing (II Corinthians 4:4). And he deceives entire nations through political leaders. In fact, God is allowing him to gather nations together for the greatest battle ever to be fought—Armageddon (Revelation 16:14,16).

During New Testament times Satan tempted Christians to lie (Acts 5:3), and to engage in immorality (I Corinthians 7:5). Paul said Satan hindered his work (I Thessalonians 2:18), using clever devices to accomplish his tasks (II Corinthians 2:11). And there is no reason to believe Satan does anything less today to hinder and harass God's people than he did in the days of the early church.

Satan is not alone in his wickedness. He has hordes of helpers—demons, the wicked angels who followed Satan in his rebellion against God. Satan's helpers are sometimes called "demons," translated "devils" in the *King James Version* (Matthew 12:24) and sometimes the devil's "angels" (Matthew 25:41; Revelation 12:7). They are also referred to as "spirits" (Mark 5:2). But whatever you call them, these servants of Satan engage in the same wicked work that the devil occupies himself with.

It is evident from Scripture that some demons are bound, unable to afflict men, whereas others are not. Peter said, God "cast them down to hell, and delivered them into chains of darkness, to be reserved unto judgment" (II Peter 2:4). Jude said essentially the same thing: "And the angels which kept not their first estate, but left their own habitation, he [God] hath reserved in everlasting chains under darkness unto the judgment of the great day" (Jude 6).

Surely these references do not apply to all the demons, for hosts of them are free to roam and afflict the saints of God, as many other Scriptures tell us plainly. But why are some of the wicked angels confined and others are not? We cannot be dogmatic on this because Scripture does not give us a definite answer. I believe, however, that those bound in the abyss are those wicked angels who cohabited with the women of the earth in Noah's day (Genesis 6:1-7). They are the ones who left their own dwelling place and committed sexual sin with the "daughters of men," producing a strange progeny called "giants." The judgment of God in response to this flagrant wickedness was the catastrophic global flood.

Demons are the devil's emissaries. They carry out his bidding just as the holy angels minister for God. This results in conflict not only with the people of God but also with the holy angels. There is spiritual war on earth and in the heavens! But God will be victorious. The ultimate and eternal destiny of all the demons will be "everlasting fire" (Matthew 25:41) in "the lake of fire and brimstone" (Revelation 20:10).

Demon possession is the condition of one or more demons taking up residence in a person's body. Just who can be possessed by demons? I believe only the unregenerate can be.

"Why can't believers be demon possessed?" you ask. I have my reasons for this conviction. First, we have no New Testament example of a believer being possessed of demons. Second, I do not believe the Holy Spirit of God, who indwells every believer, will share His residence with the devil's demons of Hell.

It is true that sometimes we may not be able to distinguish demon influence from demon possession. Certainly demons influence and afflict the redeemed, but I believe this influence must be distinguished from possession.

What about the question of exorcism? Is it possible for believers to actually cast out demons as the Lord and the apostles did? I prefer to believe that this ability was given to the apostles for that time only, for Scripture is silent about this ability in the present age. Furthermore, I for one do not wish to have such a confrontation with the devil's demons. Rather, I believe we should beseech God, in Christ's name, and in the power of the Holy Spirit, to bring deliverance to those possessed.

I feel there is an unhealthy interest in spirit beings today, especially concerning demons. True, they are real and they are wicked. However, we should not flirt or fool with the demon world, for these creatures of Hell exercise supernatural power. But neither should we label every problem people have with a demon's name or say it is the result of demon possession.

Satan gains a victory whenever we take our attention off the Holy Spirit and place it on wicked spirits. Our strength is in the Lord, so let's keep our mind stayed on Him!

How can we possibly successfully oppose Satan and his demons? Who are we against him? Paul's answer to this pressing question is, "Put on the whole armour of God" (Ephesians 6:11). That armour is Christ Himself (Romans 13:14), whom we put on, by faith, at the time of our salvation. And we are to appropriate—live out—the position we have in Him on a daily basis.

Peter, the man who fell so quickly but was restored so triumphantly (John 18:15-27; 21:15-17), gave this word of practical advice: "Be sober, be vigilant; because your adversary the devil, as a roaring lion, walketh about, seeking whom he may devour: whom resist stedfast in the faith" (I Peter 5:8,9).

Chapter Eight
What Is Man?

Where did man come from? Really, there are only two possible answers to this question. There is the humanistic answer and there is the divine answer. Or to put it another way, there is the answer of evolution and there is the answer of divine revelation—man's answer and God's answer. We will first look at man's answer to this searching question.

The theory of evolution is not always stated in the same way. Sometimes we are told man is a direct descendant of the ape. Other times people propagate the more recent view—that man and higher apes both have a common ancestry. It really doesn't matter which view we examine. Either way, man is said to have ascended from lower animals by a "perfectly natural process."

Evolution, as an explanation for man's origin, does not just refer to change in general; it pertains to a certain kind of change—change from lifeless matter to living organisms. The evolutionary view completely rules out the supernatural. It leaves no room at all for God.

According to *Evolution,* published by International Christian Crusade, "The theory of organic evolution has been defined as the hypothesis that millions of years ago lifeless matter, acted upon by natural forces, gave origin to one or more minute living organisms which have since evolved into all living and extinct plants and animals including man."

What we have described above may be called *atheistic evolution,* because it does not allow for God. However, there are some men of science and some theologians who embrace what has come to be called *theistic evolution.* That is, they believe God used the processes of evolution to do His work of creating. These people do not agree among themselves as to just how much or to what extent God was involved in the evolutionary process. They do agree, though, that *processes* were involved in bringing the world and man into existence. And they agree that the early chapters of Genesis contain extensive figurative language.

Every variety of theistic evolution seems to be an attempt to fit Scripture into the atheistic view of life. But we cannot include both viewpoints. Either we must begin with God and take His Word for what it says, or we must begin our search for an explanation of origins apart from Him.

Hard-nosed evolutionists who do not believe in God at all are certainly not impressed with the attempt at reconciliation by those who want to somehow include God's intervention and control in the evolutionary process. Julian Huxley, a respected figure among evolutionists, said that supernaturalism "runs counter to the whole of our scientific knowledge." Huxley continues in his book *Evolution in Action,* "To postulate a divine interference with these exchanges of matter and energy at a particular moment in the earth's history is both unnecessary and illogical." And certainly he is right, for either God created the world and all life, or it all evolved. We cannot accept both.

What has God said about origins, especially man's? An honest reading of Scripture allows for no type of biological evolution. "God ended his work" of creating on the seventh day, we are told in Genesis 2:2. "He spake, and it was done; he commanded, and it stood fast" (Psalm 33:9). The Bible goes into detail on how both male and female came into existence: "And the Lord God formed man of the dust of the ground, and breathed into his nostrils the breath of life; and man became a living soul . . . . And the rib, which the Lord God had taken from man, made he a woman, and brought her unto the man" (Genesis 2:7,22).

How old is the earth? How old is man? According to evolutionists, the earth is from forty million to four-and-one-half or five billion years old. Man, they say, has been around from about two hundred thousand to one million years. The haunting question is, If man has been around that long, what has he been doing? Knowledge of any civilization much earlier than the earliest cities, dated about 6,000 years before Christ, is highly uncertain.

The Bible does not specifically state how old either the earth or man is. It does tell us, though, that God did His work of creating in six days. And there is every reason to believe these were twenty-four hour, or solar, days, for in the Genesis account God restricts time. He talks about "evening" and "morning"; "first," "second," etc. And to further substantiate the twenty-four hour creative day, we can turn to Exodus 20:11. The wording of this Fourth Commandment, presenting the whole basis for Old Testament sabbath observance, becomes rather meaningless if the days were not literal twenty-four hour days. Furthermore, every other place in the Bible where the word "day" is used with a numerical adjective (such as "first"), a literal day is being spoken of. Why should it not be the same in Genesis 1 and 2?

When you think about it, there are really only two kinds of substances in the world—material and immaterial. And man is made up of both of these.

God took the "dust of the ground" and out of it "formed man" (Genesis 2:7). Out of dust man was taken, and unto dust he will return (Genesis 3:19). So God did not create man's material parts out of nothing, but He made them out of something He had previously created—dust.

After forming man out of the dust, God "breathed into his nostrils the breath of life; and man became a living soul" (Genesis 2:7). In this way God brought into being man's immaterial parts—He created them out of nothing. And strangely enough, evolution has no explanation for these immaterial aspects of man.

Whereas it may be said that man is made up of body, soul, and spirit, it is still true that his soul and his spirit are both immaterial. And man not only has a soul and a spirit, but he also has a heart (the seat of the emotions), a conscience, and a mind. These may all be viewed as functions or facets of the immaterial part of man. But for our discussion, I will let the "mind" represent the immaterial aspects of man.

Both sin against God and service for Him begin in the mind. Deeds, whether pleasing to God or displeasing to Him, are the result of what was first thought about and contemplated in the mind. Since this is true, can you see how very important our thought life is?

Man's mind—his thought processes—was affected by the Fall just as much as every other part of his being was affected. The unregenerate are "vain in their imaginations, and their foolish heart was darkened . . . .As they did not like to retain God in their knowledge, God gave them over to a reprobate mind" (Romans 1:21, 28). And what is more, Satan has "blinded the minds of them which believe not, lest the light of the glorious gospel of Christ, who is the image of God, should shine unto them" (II Corinthians 4:4). Because of this condition only the Spirit of God can bring men to repentance and faith.

But what about the mind of the person who has trusted in Christ as his Saviour? Peter tells us he needs to gird his mind (I Peter 1:13). To "gird" means to keep under control. It's true that as a man "thinketh in his heart, so is he" (Proverbs 23:7). And so our prayer, like David's, ought to be, "Let the words of my mouth, and the meditation of my heart, be acceptable in thy sight, O Lord, my strength, and my redeemer" (Psalm 19:14).

The Lord has promised that when the believer's mind is stayed on Him, the believer will be kept in perfect peace. And just how does one have his mind "stayed" on the Lord? By trusting in the Lord, according to Isaiah 26:3.

The book of Philippians is filled with

emphasis upon the mind—the thought life—of the believer. There we are told to have the mind of Christ—to be of a humble and selfless mind (Philippians 2:5-8). By prayer and supplication, God's peace will keep our heart and mind through Christ Jesus (Philippians 4:6,7).

Paul instructed the Philippian saints to think. But the instruction also listed what they were to think about. We are to think about things that are true, honest, just, pure, lovely, and of good report (Philippians 4:8). Such thinking will certainly promote and benefit the good life—try it!

It seems that little attention is given to what the Bible has to say about the believer's body. But Paul wrote that we are to present our bodies to the Lord as a living sacrifice (Romans 12:1). This is because the Holy Spirit of God dwells in the believer's body. He has made our body His holy temple (I Corinthians 6:19).

These bodies of ours are indeed "fearfully and wonderfully made" (Psalm 139:14). But we often forget that it is by means of our bodies that we serve the Lord. We sometimes forget, too, that we have only one body. And it is a sin to harm that body. Lack of proper rest, proper food, and proper care of the body hinders and hampers our work for God. Don't burn *out* for the Lord; just *burn* for Him. Discipline with respect to our bodies is equally as important, in the long run, as discipline in our spiritual life.

"God said, Let us make man in our image, after our likeness. . . . So God created man in his own image" (Genesis 1:26,27). What an awesome thought! We were created to be like God!

But one thing is certain: the image of God in man is not physical. That is, man does not look like God. God is a spirit and therefore He does not possess a physical body (John 4:24). Then, too, the fact that God made man *and* woman tells us the image and likeness are not physical, for He could not look like both.

If the image is not physical it must be spiritual. But in what way is man like God in the spiritual aspect? Surely this does not mean man is in any sense divine. No, what it means is that the likeness of man to God includes personality. Man has personality, intellect, emotion, and will. God does, too, as we have seen in chapter 2 of this book. The Creator could not possibly be impersonal, since His creature is personal.

The image seems also to be related somehow to the responsibility God gave Adam and Eve to have dominion over the earth and its inhabitants. God is sovereign; and so He gave to man the right to rule (Genesis 1:26-28). However, because of sin a curse was placed upon the earth. But the responsibility was not lost. Even after the Fall and the Noahic flood man still possessed this right to rule (Genesis 9:6,7). Thus in function there is a likeness between God and man.

Too, man's likeness to God is related to knowledge, righteousness, and holiness. We know this is true because in the New Testament we are told that in Christ, who is the Image of the invisible God, these characteristics are restored to man (Romans 8:29). In other words, when man sinned he lost the original knowledge, righteousness, and holiness which he had as he came from the hands of God. But in Christ these are restored. The new man, Paul told the Colossians, "is renewed in knowledge after the image of him that created him" (Colossians 3:10).

Man's likeness to God seems also to include immortality. Of course, only God possesses this as an essential quality (I Timothy 6:15,16). But man was given immortality as an endowment from God. Before the Fall there was no death. But after Adam and Eve sinned, "death passed upon all men" (Romans 5:12). Now again, because of Christ's death and resurrection, all will live eternally—some to everlasting life and some to everlasting damnation (John 5:28,29).

There is great significance in the truth of man's likeness to God. In fact, all the exhortations in the Epistles are based upon this truth. The believer is God's representative on earth. Therefore it is his solemn duty to live in such a way that he will be a good testimony for Christ to those who have not yet been renewed in

His image.

Because of sin, man, who was made in the image of God, is so marred that only God's grace can restore him. And the restoration is not merely to what the first Adam was before the Fall, but to much more in Christ, the last Adam.

"What is the chief end of man?" asks the old Westminster Shorter Catechism. That is indeed a question of tremendous import. And it calls for an answer. The Catechism goes on to answer its own question: "The chief end of man is to glorify God and to enjoy Him forever."

How does one glorify God? By obeying His Word. To "glorify" is to honor, praise, and adore. And only as we submit to the authority of God, the Father, the Son, and the Holy Spirit, as made known in the Word, can we glorify Him.

God made man. He made him from dust and breathed into his nostrils the breath of life. In His own likeness and after His image He formed man. To be sure, the image has been marred; but it has not been destroyed. Through our regenerated lives and with our redeemed lips God would have us praise Him, love Him, and serve Him.

Chapter Nine
The Truth about Sin

Sin is taking sides against God. That sounds terrible, doesn't it? But it's true. Yes, when we sin we miss the mark God has set for us. And we must not forget that when we miss the right mark we hit a wrong mark. Sin is not only failing to do the right (James 4:17), it is also succeeding in doing the wrong. To "be a friend of the world," James wrote, is to be "the enemy of God" (James 4:4). If that isn't siding against God, I don't know what is.

Certainly sin is lack of consciousness of God. It springs from selfishness and is a transgression of the law. But most seriously, sin is transgression against God; it is failure to conform to His character. God is the only standard by which men and their actions are to be judged. His character is, of course, revealed in the Bible, His Word. "Ye shall be holy: for I the Lord your God am holy" (Leviticus 19:2; see also I Peter 1:16). This is God's pronouncement.

In recent days, the death of absolutes has occurred, as far as many are concerned. No longer is it considered wise to think in terms of right and wrong.

But God hasn't changed, has He? No, He still hates sin. He always has and He always will. But what does "sin" refer to? In God's Word "sin" speaks of a state of being as well as of specific acts. All men are sinners, and all men sin. In fact, man sins *because* he is a sinner.

The Bible leaves the question of the origin of sin with Satan. It traces it back no further. Therefore we would do well to respect God's silence on the matter. To probe further is to run the risk of raising more problems than we can solve. Someday we will understand fully. But until then we should trust and wait, knowing God's ways are better and far beyond ours.

Let us go back to the garden of Eden. God had placed the first human pair in that place of pleasure and delight. Though we are not sure, the place was probably located in the highlands of Armenia near the Tigris and Euphrates Rivers in Persia.

Wherever it was, the garden constituted a perfect environment. Both Adam and Eve, as well as all else that had come from God's creative hand, were pronounced "good" by God. But even though the garden was perfect, it was there that the devil induced our first parents to do what he had done—to act independently of God and His will. And of course, such independence is the basic factor of all sin.

The first man and woman had been given only one prohibition along with their many privileges (Genesis 2:15-20). They were not to eat of the fruit of the Tree of the Knowledge of Good and Evil. But Satan, speaking through the serpent, succeeded in influencing Eve to doubt God's goodness and His right to restrict her and her husband (Genesis 3:1-3). He then flatly denied God's Word and in reality called God a liar (Genesis 3:4). Eve yielded to his trickery and ate of the forbidden fruit. She then gave some fruit to Adam, who also ate, although he was not deceived (I Timothy 2:14).

That is how sin began. Satan committed the first sin in the universe, and then our first parents followed in his path on this planet. It could be that sin always existed as an abstract principle by virtue of the eternal existence of a holy God. Not until Satan sinned, however, did it find expression in a specific act.

Based upon what we know about God from His Word we can say that God allowed sin in His plan because by this means He could and would bring the most glory to His name. However, we must remember that in no way does God ever accept the blame for the acts of sin committed by either angels or men. The sinner is always held responsible for his own sin.

Few people would deny that man is not as good as he ought to be. But many would doubt and/or deny that there is a definite relation between Adam's sin and ours, between Adam and his posterity. The truth is, God has declared that there is a definite connection between the first man and woman and all other human beings. And we have to realize that the good life is not even possible until a person sees himself as God sees him—a son of Adam, participating in Adam's sin and therefore a guilty sinner.

Just why does man sin? What is it that prompts him to rebel against God? Is it his environment? To be sure, this old world is not a friend of grace. The evil surrounding us does indeed contribute to our sinning. But we can't blame environment for sin. Adam and Eve lived in a perfect environment, and yet they sinned. And after the future thousand years of peace when Jesus Christ Himself will reign on the earth, men will again rebel against God (Revelation 20:7-10). No, the problem is much more than environmental.

According to Scripture, man sins because he has what may be called a sin nature, which he inherited from his parents. They inherited it from their parents, and they from theirs, all the way back to Adam. But what, exactly, is a sin nature? It is that inherent drive, bent, capacity and desire to sin that is within everyone. The Bible refers to this inborn inclination to sin as "the flesh," as opposed to the spirit, and as the "old man," in opposition to the "new man." There can be no mistaking it—Scripture teaches that we are *naturally* "children of wrath" (Ephesians 2:3). This is what Jeremiah the prophet meant when he said, "the heart is deceitful above all things" (Jeremiah 17:9).

As we have seen, the first Adam and his wife Eve did not have a sin nature when they came into the world; however, they received one when they ate of the forbidden fruit. And then, without any intent on their part, yet without the ability to do otherwise, they passed that evil inclination on to their offspring.

There is still another side to the truth about sin and the relationship between Adam's sin and ours. The Apostle Paul expressed it clearly in these words: "Wherefore, as by one man sin entered into the world, and death by sin; and so death passed upon all men, for that all have sinned" (Romans 5:12). That is a profound statement. Read that Scripture again, and ponder its meaning.

The "one man" spoken of is obviously Adam. The "world" is the world of men—"all men." Through the one man, Adam, sin entered this world. That is the story of Genesis, chapter 3. But notice what else

Paul tells us here. As a result of sin, death also entered the world. And what is more, death "passed upon all men." Why did that happen? Why should death come to all just because one man sinned? The divine answer is given in the last part of the verse: "For that all have sinned." This is more literally rendered, "All sinned." What this means is that even though only one man, Adam, disobeyed God and ate the forbidden fruit, in another sense everybody ever to descend from that first man also sinned. As far as God is concerned we also ate, disobeying Him. You see, Adam was both the natural and the divinely appointed federal head of the entire human race. When he sinned the whole race of mankind sinned, because the race was in him.

Some may try to argue with God, accusing Him of being unfair. "I didn't disobey God in the garden," they cry. But God knows, and we know, too, that had we been there that day, we *would* have disobeyed God.

So, the whole world stands guilty before God. Guilty not just because all inherited a sin nature from their parents and therefore they commit acts of sin, but also because God views all as having sinned in Adam.

Immediately after Adam and Eve ate of the forbidden fruit God announced the penalties for this flagrant disobedience. First of all he spoke to the serpent: "Because thou hast done this, thou art cursed above all cattle, and above every beast of the field; upon thy belly shalt thou go, and dust shalt thou eat all the days of thy life" (Genesis 3:14).

God then told Satan, who had spoken through the serpent, "I will put enmity between thee and the woman, and between thy seed and her seed; it shall bruise thy head, and thou shalt bruise his heel" (Genesis 3:15). This speaks of the Redeemer who would deliver man from the power of sin and would crush Satan once and for all.

Eve was told, "I will greatly multiply thy sorrow and thy conception; in sorrow thou shalt bring forth children; and thy desire shall be to thy husband, and he shall rule over thee" (Genesis 3:16).

Finally, God told Adam, "Cursed is the ground for thy sake; in sorrow shalt thou eat of it all the days of thy life; Thorns also and thistles shall it bring forth to thee; and thou shalt eat the herb of the field; In the sweat of thy face shalt thou eat bread, till thou return unto the ground; for out of it wast thou taken: for dust thou art, and unto dust shalt thou return" (Genesis 3:17-19).

Three forms of death came about when Adam and Eve sinned. God had previously said of the Tree of the Knowledge of Good and Evil, "In the day that thou eatest thereof thou shalt surely die" (Genesis 2:17). And Adam and Eve did die. Physical death began to set in the instant they sinned; and finally it took its toll, as we can see from the obituary column in Genesis 5.

Our first parents died spiritually, too. By this I mean that they were separated from God. We know this because of the attempts they made to hide from God and accuse each other.

Eternal death also became a reality when Adam and Eve sinned. Eternal death is the extension of spiritual death that occurs when God's remedy for sin is rejected by man. It denotes eternal separation from God, and it came about as a result of Adam's sin.

The truth about sin paints a dark, ugly picture. The things God's Word says about sin do not appeal to man or compliment him. What happened in the garden when Eve and then Adam disobeyed God represents the most tragic occurrence in the history of the world. That one act of disobedience, in which all participated, made necessary the death of Christ, for one basic truth about sin is that it demands a Saviour. But salvation from sin and its horrible penalties has been provided in God's Son, the Saviour of men. All who trust in Him receive forgiveness (Ephesians 1:7).

Chapter Ten
On Being Born Again

The expression "born again" is being heard from unexpected sources today. It is rather common to hear about men and women of great fame and fortune who have been "born again." It used to be that only those who had truly experienced the Biblical new birth talked about being born again. But that is not true anymore. Not too long ago a Gallup poll revealed that one out of every three Americans, and as many as half of all Protestants, actually claim to be "born again."

For Bible-believing Christians, to be "born again" is more than just a trite phrase. It is to be saved from eternal Hell. It is to become a member of God's family, to be rightly related to God through the Lord Jesus Christ.

From start to finish salvation—being born again—is the work of God. God must make the first move if ever He and man are to be reconciled. The truth is, man in his natural state can't make any move toward God. He is dead in trespasses and sins. There is nothing in man which can respond to God. Before we can ever understand in any way God's work of salvation, we must first understand how totally lost and far from God all men really are.

God's picture of the unsaved man as presented in the Bible is not very complimentary. There we are told man is "lost" (Luke 19:10), "condemned" (John 3:18), under "the wrath of God" (John 3:36), "dead in trespasses and sins" (Ephesians 2:1), a son "of disobedience" (Ephesians 2:2), under the "power of darkness" (Colossians 1:13), "blinded" by Satan (II Corinthians 4:4), and "unprofitable" (Romans 3:12).

Who dares to deny the fact that outside Christ man is a guilty rebel against God, without any ability to be reconciled to God? It is because of this, you see, that God must make the first move to save man. And He did indeed make that first move.

Man's sin did not come as a surprise to God. He knew all about it and even allowed its entrance into the world. We know this because Scripture tells us about God's eternal plan to solve the problem which sin created. The problem was, How can God remain holy and just, yet at the same time forgive the sinner and allow the sinner into His very presence? After all, God is absolutely holy, and that means He cannot tolerate sin.

In eternity past, before time began and before sin entered the world, God the Father instituted a plan of redemption. That eternal plan centered in the death of His Son. Peter said Christ "was foreordained before the foundation of the world" to be our Redeemer (I Peter 1:20). He also told the crowd on the day of Pentecost that the Saviour was "delivered by the determinate counsel and foreknowledge of God" (Acts 2:23). What was done to Christ on the cross was by the Father's hand "determined before to be done" (Acts 4:28). Yes, Christ the Lamb was "slain from the foundation of the world" (Revelation 13:8).

God the Father not only designed a plan for man's salvation, but He also chose individuals to be in Christ "before the foundation of the world" (Ephesians 1:4). The Bible tells believers they were "elect according to the foreknowledge of God the Father" (I Peter 1:2). Those whom God foreknew, Paul declared, "he also did predestinate to be conformed to the image of his Son" (Romans 8:29). "God hath from the beginning chosen you to salvation," Paul told the Thessalonians (II Thessalonians 2:13). The Lord Jesus Himself told His disciples that "all that the Father giveth me shall come to me" (John 6:37). That has been God the Father's work—to institute the plan of salvation and to give individuals to the Son.

God the Father sent His Son into the world just at the right time to suffer and die, making provision for man's salvation (Galatians 4:4,5). On the cross God the Son gave Himself as the final offering for sin. He lived an altogether sinless life, yet in His death on the cross He bore our sins (I Peter 2:24). The Saviour was actually *made* sin for us, even though He knew no sin, just so "that we might be made the righteousness of God in him" (II Corinthians 5:21).

God the Son's work was to die, to give Himself as a ransom, so that we might be born again. He died as our Substitute. He died not only for our good and benefit, but He also took our place. Even "while we were yet sinners, Christ died for us" (Romans 5:8). Yes, in Jesus Christ, God the Father reconciled "the world unto himself, not imputing their trespasses unto them" (II Corinthians 5:19).

The third member of the Godhead also has an indispensable work to perform in the salvation of a soul. It is the Holy Spirit's work to bring conviction of sin to the sinner, to show him that Christ is the only Saviour, and to enable him to trust in Christ alone for salvation.

Before His death Christ told His disciples He would send the Holy Spirit to continue the work He had begun. God the Spirit, the Saviour said, would "reprove the world of sin, and of righteousness, and of judgment" (John 16:8). That is, He would provide man with faultless proof of the facts concerning sin, righteousness, and judgment.

Jesus also told Nicodemus that man must be born "of the Spirit" to enter the kingdom of God (John 3:5). Only by the "renewing of the Holy Ghost" can a person be born again (Titus 3:5).

Just how does the Spirit of God convict and draw men to Christ? Through the Word of God. The Holy Spirit uses the Word of God, dispersed by the man of God, to bring men to the Son of God so that they might become the children of God.

But is that all there is to this business of being born again? How does man fit into this whole picture? What is man's responsibility when it comes to being born again?

Over and over again the Bible calls upon all men to believe on the Lord Jesus Christ and be saved. Never is man told to better himself through self-improvement. He is not even told to give up anything, except confidence in himself, in order to be saved. This is not to say a person's life will not change when he becomes a child of God. It will, according to II Corinthians 5:17. But we are talking about what, precisely, a man must do to be born again.

There is only one way of salvation for all people everywhere. And that one and only way is through the Lord Jesus Christ. The question is, How do we get to Him? How does He become our Saviour? A person must *believe on the Lord Jesus Christ* to be saved, as Paul and Silas told the Philippian jailer in response to his question, "What must I do to be saved?" (Acts 16:30,31).

The Lord Jesus told Nicodemus, "Whosoever believeth in him ["the Son of man which is in heaven" (John 3:13)] should not perish, but have eternal life" (John 3:15). The Apostle John wrote, "But as many as received him [Christ], to them gave he power to become the sons of God, even to them that believe on his name" (John 1:12). Here we see that "receive" and "believe" mean the same thing.

Believing in Christ alone as Saviour is in no way working to earn salvation. No, faith does not involve doing something, but simply receiving something—eternal life. When we receive a gift from someone we have not earned it. And when we receive salvation by faith, we are not working for it. Nowhere in the Bible is faith or trust ever viewed as a contribution which man makes toward his salvation. For it is not man's faith which saves him. Christ alone saves. But by means of faith man lays hold of Christ and appropriates the salvation He provided. And it is always in response to the Holy Spirit's work that a man trusts Christ as his Saviour.

What does it really mean to "believe on the Lord Jesus Christ"? Is belief that a man named Jesus lived and died enough to be saved? A person would be a fool to deny such a well-established fact of history. So it is obvious that merely giving intellectual assent to historical facts does not bring salvation to anyone.

If believing in Christ as Saviour means more than just accepting historical facts about Him, what does it mean? The gospel, the good news of salvation, includes three essentials. First, man is a guilty sinner, under the condemnation of God. Second, Christ died as the sinner's Substitute, satisfying every demand of God's offended righteousness. And third, the guilty sinner must accept Christ, trusting Him alone as his Substitute for his sin. All who in childlike faith trust in the Lord Jesus Christ will be saved, will receive eternal life, will be born again.

But someone may say, "What about repentance? Must not man repent of his sin to be born again?" In the Bible the word "repent" means to change the mind. It involves an about-face. No one believes in Christ alone as Saviour without repenting, for he has changed his mind from self-sufficiency to faith in Christ. And all who truly repent, who truly change their minds about themselves and the Saviour, do believe in Him alone for salvation. Repentance and faith are two sides of the same truth (Acts 20:21).

God's gift of salvation to the sinner is full and free. By *full* I mean it is complete. Nothing need be, or can be, added to it; nothing can be taken away from it. The very moment the repentant sinner places his trust in the Saviour he receives everlasting life. He actually partakes of the divine nature (II Peter 1:4).

By *free* I mean this great salvation is a gift to all who will receive it. However, it was not free as far as God was concerned. Salvation was extremely costly to God. God Himself came to earth in the person of Jesus Christ and died in the sinner's place. Now, through His priceless blood, we can be born again (I Peter 1:18,19).

The hymn writer must have had in mind the great truths of Scripture that describe God's salvation of sinners when he penned these words:

Salvation full, salvation free–
The price was paid on Calvary.
O, weary wanderer, come and see–
It is for you; it is for me.

Why has God saved us? The primary reason is so that we might serve Him and in doing so bring honor and glory to His name. The redeemed are tokens of His grace and through them, God desires to display His grace to the world. And so we should submit to God and obey Him as a sign of our thanks and as a demonstration of His marvelous grace.

Chapter Eleven
The Church and Churches

Criticism of the old and a demand for change seem to be two outstanding features of the church these days. A number of innovative ideas are being introduced that greatly affect the nature and function of the church. Why is this? What has happened to the church? Are the criticisms and cries for change justified? What does the Bible teach us about the church?

We first need to realize that in the New Testament there is teaching about both Christ's body, the church, and local churches. We must keep these two aspects of the Scriptural teaching distinct in our minds, for failure to differentiate between these two and the truth concerning each can result in great confusion.

The church is very important to God. Teaching about the church is not some isolated truth of Scripture, but the body of Christ and the local church, as well, occupy a large place in God's Word and in His plan.

The Lord Jesus loves the church. He gave Himself for it, as we see in Ephesians 5:25. He is coming back to take the church to be with Him forever (John 14:1-3). And just as surely as the Holy Spirit of God indwells every child of God, He indwells the New Testament church (I Corinthians 6:19; 3:17).

Something new and wonderful took place on the day of Pentecost. The record is in Acts 2. In fulfillment of Christ's promise that He would build His church (Matthew 16:18) and that His own would be baptized with the Holy Spirit (Acts 1:5), the Spirit came upon that company of believers gathered in Jerusalem. "And they were all filled with the Holy Ghost, and began to speak with other tongues, as the Spirit gave them utterance" (Acts 2:4).

Some time after that spectacular experience Peter recalled how God had dealt with him about reaching out beyond the bounds of Judaism to the Gentiles. After considerable persuasion, Peter finally went to the Gentiles in the home of Cornelius. In reflecting on that momentous experience, he said the Spirit fell on the Gentiles just as He had on the Jews earlier (Acts 11:15). When the Spirit came in this new and distinct way Peter remembered how the Lord Jesus had promised the baptism of the Holy Spirit (verse 16). In other words, he related what happened on the day of Pentecost and in the home of Cornelius to what the Lord had promised (Acts 1:5).

The church is Christ's body, according to Ephesians 1:22,23 and Colossians 1:24. This church was formed by the baptism of the Holy Spirit, Paul told the Corinthians in I Corinthians 12:12,13.

There you have it—the church was born on the day of Pentecost, it was formed by the baptism of the Spirit, and it is called the body of Christ. This great company is composed of all those who, since its beginning, have acknowledged their sin and trusted Christ alone as their Saviour. From the day of Pentecost until the present, all who respond in faith to Christ are made members of the body of Christ. All who are born again are therefore made one in Christ.

The body of Christ is not restricted to church members of any particular denomination. Neither does race, color, or even creed determine its boundaries. There is but one qualification, one requirement, for membership in the body of Christ. That one essential, without which one cannot be a member, is the new birth. This is because it is at the very moment of faith in Christ as Saviour that the Holy Spirit of God takes the believing sinner and brings him into vital union with Christ, the Head of the church. The same Spirit also relates the trusting soul to all the other members of the body. He makes them all members one of another, and together they all "are one body" (I Corinthians 12:12).

We must not forget that all the members of Christ's body need each other. Paul's comparison of the body of Christ with the human body is indeed significant. Just as there are many parts of a human body, yet there is only one body; so in the body of Christ there are many members, but only one body. Some parts of our physical bodies are not as prominent or as indispensable as other members. Yet each member is necessary and important to the proper function of the body. So it is in the body of Christ. Not all the members have the same function, but all are needed.

One important thing to remember is that Christ is the Head of the church. Scripture makes this abundantly clear (Ephesians 1:22,23; 5:23,24; Colossians 1:18). As the Head Christ provides guidance and direction to the body. And He is in the position of authority over the church. He is her Lord! He is to be obeyed! We need to individually and personally submit to Christ's sovereign lordship if we really respect His position as Head of the body. But you may say, "How do we know what His instructions to us as members of the body are?" They are given to us in the Word of God.

Christ loved the church so much that He gave Himself for it (Ephesians 5:25). And because the Saviour loves the church He provides spiritual nourishment and comfort for every member through His written Word (Ephesians 5:29).

Between Lebanon and Allentown, Pennsylvania, there is a tourist attraction called "Miniature America." And it is just that. On a very small scale every facet of American life is portrayed there in a beautiful and accurate way.

Every local church ought to be a "Miniature Body of Christ." No one church in any given location is the body of Christ. Not even all local churches all over the world taken together equal the body of Christ. No, the body of Christ, as we have seen, includes *all* who are born again, whether they are members of a local church or not. But it is God's great desire that each local body of believers who meet for worship, instruction, and evangelism, be modeled after the body of Christ.

No doubt about it—the local church has a high priority in the New Testament. It is God's means of carrying out His program in this age. God views it as "the pillar and ground of the truth" (I Timothy 3:15). Nowhere in Scripture are we given the right to forsake the local church and replace it with other institutions and organizations. True, many times and in many ways the church has failed. The solution, however, is not to replace the church, but to call it back to the Word and its God-given responsibility.

Our view of the local church, concerning both precept and practice, comes from what is recorded in the New Testament. Let me explain. By *precept* I mean what we are actually told to do, the instructions of Scripture. By *practice* I mean what the early Christians did as an example to us. From the commands and the record of early practice we build our doctrine of the local church.

Just what constitutes a local church? How about "where two or three are gathered together" in Christ's name (Matthew 18:20). Is that a local church? Or a Bible college or seminary—are these the same as a local church?

Several things must be included in a good definition of the local New Testament church. These will be true regardless of whether the church has a denominational label or not.

In the New Testament each local church had as its *purpose* the public worship of God, edification of the saints, and the spread of the gospel. It was for these reasons that the churches existed.

Organization also characterized the New Testament church. There were planned meetings (Acts 20:7); there was corporate discipline (I Corinthians 5); there were money-raising projects (II Corinthians 8; 9); there were leaders who had the rule over the flock (Hebrews 13:7,17). Granted, the organization was simple; but it developed as the need arose.

Human leadership also marked the New Testament church. The pastor is one who is gifted by the Spirit (Ephesians 4:11) to provide spiritual food for God's people.

The one who does this is also called an "elder" (I Peter 5:1-4). The terms "elder" and "bishop" are applied to the same person (the pastor) in Titus 1:5-7. Again in Acts 20:17-28 Paul calls the elders (pastors) of the church at Ephesus "overseers" or "bishops." But no matter what you call these men, they are told to do the work of a shepherd—they are to feed the flock of God.

There were also deacons in the New Testament church. They are first referred to in Acts 6. Their qualifications are given in I Timothy 3. Although all of God's people are called upon to serve the Lord, deacons do so in an official capacity.

Another essential in defining the local church had to do with the *ordinances*. Most evangelical Protestants believe the New Testament presents two of these to be observed by God's people—believer's baptism and the Lord's Supper. Some Christians also include foot washing. Those who reject foot washing as an ordinance do so for two reasons. First, they believe its defense is weak. Second, they understand our Lord's practice and teaching of foot washing to be explained culturally.

There are, to be sure, differences of opinion over specifics regarding these four essentials to a local church. But they are indispensable if we are to understand the New Testament concept of the local church.

God has saved us by His marvelous grace so that we might serve Him. As His children, we are given the privilege and the responsibility to work for Him both in the local church and in the body of Christ.

To make it possible for His children to function in a fruitful manner, God has, by His Holy Spirit, given them abilities to serve Him. In the New Testament these are called *spiritual gifts.* In three major passages we are given lists of these (I Corinthians 12; Romans 12; Ephesians 4). However, not necessarily all of God's enablements for service are named in these lists.

"How may I know what my ability or abilities are?" you ask. Many of God's people spend much time in frustration and idleness waiting to discover their gift. The far better thing to do is to get busy and involved in God's work, especially through a Bible-believing, Bible-preaching local church. As we work, God will make clear to us what our abilities are and where and how we can best use them.

In God's family there are no little or insignificant people. Every task in the work of God is of tremendous significance. And everyone in the household of faith is important and of genuine worth and value to God. Take a look at the list of names in the closing verses of the book of Colossians. Most of these saints of God are rarely mentioned in the New Testament. By all human standards they are nobodies. And yet they were tremendously important to God, to His work, and to His servant Paul.

Every believer has the same standing before God, and each one is urgently needed in the work of God. As we serve Him in the capacity He has placed us in, we will experience more fully the joy of the good life.

Chapter Twelve
Looking Ahead

Why are crystal ball gazers and other kinds of fortune-tellers gaining such popularity these days? There seems to be an unprecedented desire to peer into the unknown. Predictions are being made every day about what is going to happen in the future. So-called prophets abound. But most of their prophecies are wrong.

The Bible, too, is full of prophecy. However, much of what it predicted has already come to pass. And the prophecy which is yet unfulfilled will in due time also be fulfilled. We may be sure of this because God does not lie—He *cannot* lie.

End times and future events have recently become topics of much discussion among Christians. World conditions and events, especially in the Middle East, have drawn attention to Biblical prophecy. There is considerable disagreement among students of prophecy as to the relationship between current happenings in the world and Bible prophecy. There is also much disagreement concerning the precise order of future events. Yet in spite of these differences, there is a general concensus that we are living in the last days.

Led by the Spirit of God, the prophets foretold Christ's first coming. The Saviour came as had been promised, even though many had given up all hope. While He was on the earth, Christ told His followers He would die at the hands of the very people He came to redeem. And He did. The Saviour also said He would be raised again from the dead and would ascend back to the Father. And indeed, He was raised and He did ascend back to the Father. With equal fervor and clarity Christ also said He would come again. And just as surely as Christ came the first time, He will come again.

When Christ came the first time it was in meekness and lowliness. Imagine it—God the Son humbling Himself to be born a baby to a humble virgin, with only a cattle's trough for His cradle. But when He comes again, He will come with power and great glory.

Actually, the New Testament teaches that there will be two aspects of Christ's return. In a sense He will come twice in the future. Here is what I mean. First, He will come at the sound of a heavenly trumpet (I Corinthians 15:52) and with the shout of Michael the archangel (I Thessalonians 4:16). All who are in

Christ will at that time meet Him in the air and be caught up with Him into Heaven. The dead in Christ will be raised first (I Thessalonians 4:14), and then those who are still alive in Christ will be changed "in a moment, in the twinkling of an eye" (I Corinthians 15:52).

The return described above is often called the rapture of the church. It is the next great event on God's calendar of events for the future. It is the imminent hope of the child of God, for the trumpet could sound and the shout of the archangel could be heard at any time. Christ could come at any moment. We do not know when Christ will come, but we do know He *will* come. What a blessed hope that is! It certainly calls us to be prepared, for He could come today. Are we ready?

What will happen after Christ takes us to be with Himself? What will take place on the earth? What will be going on in Heaven?

Apparently rather soon after the rapture an outstanding political leader will become prominent and will sign a covenant or an agreement with the leaders of the state of Israel, promising to protect that little nation from all her hostile enemies.

When the covenant between the great political leader and Israel is signed (Daniel 9:27) the period our Lord called the Great Tribulation will begin

(Matthew 24:21). According to Daniel's prophecy this time of unprecedented trouble will last seven years (Daniel 9:24-27). During that time the awful wrath of God will be poured out upon the earth and men. Details about this time are given in Revelation 6—18.

Believers making up the body of Christ will not be on the earth during this time. They will have been raptured—caught up to be with the Lord—before the Great Tribulation ever begins. God does not want His children to experience this time of wrath (Revelation 6:17; cf. I Thessalonians 5:9), so He will keep them out of the Tribulation period (Revelation 3:10). Furthermore, the divine purpose of the future Great Tribulation as seen in Scripture is always related to Israel, not to the church. The period is even called "the time of Jacob's trouble" (Jeremiah 30:7).

During that terrible time multitudes will turn in faith to Christ for salvation (Revelation 7:9-14; 14:1-5). They will, of course, be redeemed just as everyone else has been redeemed— through the blood of Christ, the Lamb. "But how," you may ask, "will they hear the gospel?" God will have witnesses upon the earth even in that time. The witnesses will include the 144,000 spoken of in Revelation 7:4 as well as other faithful servants.

But what will be going on in Heaven among the raptured saints during that same period of time? There will first be the "judgment seat of Christ" (I Corinthians 3:11-15; II Corinthians 5:10). All the church saints will appear before the Lord at this judgment. They will be there *because* they are believers, not in order to determine whether or not they are. The issue before God's people at that time will not be concerning their salvation, but their service. Each one will give an account of himself to God, and will lose or gain rewards depending upon the kind of service he gave to the Lord while he was living on earth.

It is possible to build our Christian lives on the solid foundation of the Saviour. This is described as gold, silver, and precious stones. Or we may build upon self —wood, hay, and stubble (I Corinthians 3:12,13). Christ Himself will be the judge. He will reveal the truth about our lives and service. All hypocrisy will be stripped away.

While the Great Tribulation is taking place on the earth there will also be "the marriage of the Lamb" in Heaven (Revelation 19:7). Like the last phase of an Oriental wedding, this feast will be the great consummation of the marriage relationship between Christ and His bride, the church.

After the time of the Great Tribulation, Christ will return again. At that time He will come down to the earth, and His feet will touch the Mount of Olives. Coming with Him will be the redeemed saints and the holy angels (Matthew 24:27-31; Revelation 19:11-21). This will not be a secret coming or a meeting of the saints with Christ in the air so He can catch them away. Rather, He will come in power and glory to rule and reign on the earth.

Before Christ's kingdom is established on the earth, all the saints who died before the church was born at Pentecost and those who died during the Great Tribulation will be raised from the dead (Daniel 12:2; John 5:28,29; Revelation 20:4-6). These, along with those who were raptured seven years earlier, will rule and reign with Christ.

More judgments will take place at this coming of Christ. Living Israelites will be judged (Ezekiel 20:34-38; Matthew 25: 1-30). All the unbelievers among them will be cut off, whereas the believers will be allowed to enter the millennium. Living Gentiles will also be judged (Joel 3:1,2; Matthew 25:31-46). The result will be that those on the right, the redeemed, will enter the kingdom; those on the left, the unredeemed, will be cast into everlasting fire. Satan and all the wicked angels will also be judged, but not until later.

When God has finished judging the living, and His Son has put down all existing rule and authority, He will then establish His kingdom on the earth. Imagine it! Finally there will be peace on the earth. The long-promised and long-awaited earthly kingdom of the Messiah will be established. The Prince of Peace, Christ

Jesus Himself, will be here. David's greater Son will rule over the whole world with a rod of iron. And His throne will be in Jerusalem. This kingdom will be the fulfillment of the promises made to the people of Israel so long ago (II Samuel 7:1-17).

Only the righteous, those rightly related to Christ, the King, will be allowed to enter the millennial kingdom (Isaiah 60:21). Holiness will characterize the time (Zechariah 14:20,21). Truth will prevail at last (Psalm 85:10,11). The Holy Spirit will be poured out in all His fullness (Joel 2:28,29). Peace will prevail because all the kingdoms of the world will be under the rule and reign of Christ (Isaiah 11). Perfect justice will be administered to everyone (Isaiah 42:1-4). The curse placed upon the earth because of man's sin will be lifted (Isaiah 11:6-9). Social, as well as political, and even religious, oppression will be eliminated (Isaiah 14:3-6; Zechariah 9:11,12). Great prosperity will sweep the earth (Isaiah 35:1,2; Amos 9:13,14). God's presence will be fully recognized in that day (Ezekiel 37:27,28).

"How will all this be possible?" you ask. First, the literal presence of the Lord Jesus Christ Himself, reigning from His throne, will make it possible. Also, Satan will be bound for the entire millennial reign (Revelation 20:1-3). That old dragon will be cast into the bottomless pit and chained there to await his final judgment.

No one will enter the earthly kingdom who is not rightly related to the King. But children will be born during that 1000-year period to those who are still in their earthly bodies. And they will be born in sin just like every other member of Adam's race. Their wickedness will be suppressed, however. They will not be allowed to exhibit any rebellion against Christ.

You may be asking, "What will happen after the 1000-year reign of perfect peace on the earth?" The Bible gives us a clear answer to that question. Satan will be loosed after the 1000 years. And he will be successful in deceiving many, many people. He will gather these together in battle against the people of God. But fire will come down from Heaven and devour the enemies of God (Revelation 20:8,9). Satan will then be cast into the Lake of Fire to be tormented forever and ever (Revelation 20:10).

Then there will be what Scripture calls the Great White Throne Judgment (Revelation 20:11). All the unsaved of all the ages will appear at this judgment. This judgment will not be to determine whether or not the people there have the correct credentials to enter Heaven. Rather, it will be to demonstrate or to prove that they *do not* have such credentials. All who appear at the Great White Throne Judgment will not have their names written in the Book of Life. Therefore, they will be cast into the Lake of Fire to be tormented forever and ever (Revelation 20:15).

Every human being will exist forever. Not all will experience the same kind of life throughout the endless ages of eternity; but all will experience an endless life. Therefore, an understanding of eternity and the proper preparation for it should be of utmost concern to every person.

Reports of recent studies made to determine whether there is, in fact, life after this life have doubtlessly removed the fear of death for many people. The question is, Are such reports grounds for believing that no one should fear death and what follows? According to a number of these studies, there is a being of light, who forgives and accepts all, awaiting everyone after death. The reports indicate that there is no judgment or eternal punishment for anyone.

These finds from those who are said to have had out-of-the-body experiences reveal some rather glaring contradictions with what the Bible teaches. Of course, none of those interviewed had really experienced an irreversible loss of vital functions. They had not been resurrected from the dead but were merely resuscitated or in some way revived. They were dying, but they were not really dead. It is interesting, too, that such an out-of-the-body experience can affect even people who are healthy and very much alive.

Regardless of what the reports say these "dead" people experienced or why they experienced it, the Word of God is very clear in its teaching about life after death.

Those who have never trusted Christ alone as their personal Saviour must eventually suffer an eternal torment in the Lake of Fire. At death the unsaved go to Hades (often translated "hell"), a place of conscious temporary confinement, until they appear at the Great White Throne Judgment (Revelation 20:11-15). Then these people will experience an eternal separation from the Lord (II Thessalonians 1:9). They will be in torment forever in Hell, the Lake of Fire (Revelation 14:11). Hell was prepared for the devil and his angels, yet all who refuse salvation in Christ will share that awful place with them.

For all those who know Christ as their personal Saviour there is the promise that they will be in the very presence of God at the instant of death (II Corinthians 5:1,8; Philippians 1:23). They will be made like Him and will be with Him forever (I John 3:2; I Thessalonians 4:17). All the effects of sin will be removed in the new Heaven and the new earth. And the heavenly city, the New Jerusalem, will be the abode of God's people forever and forever (Revelation 21:10).

Then the good life will be fully realized!